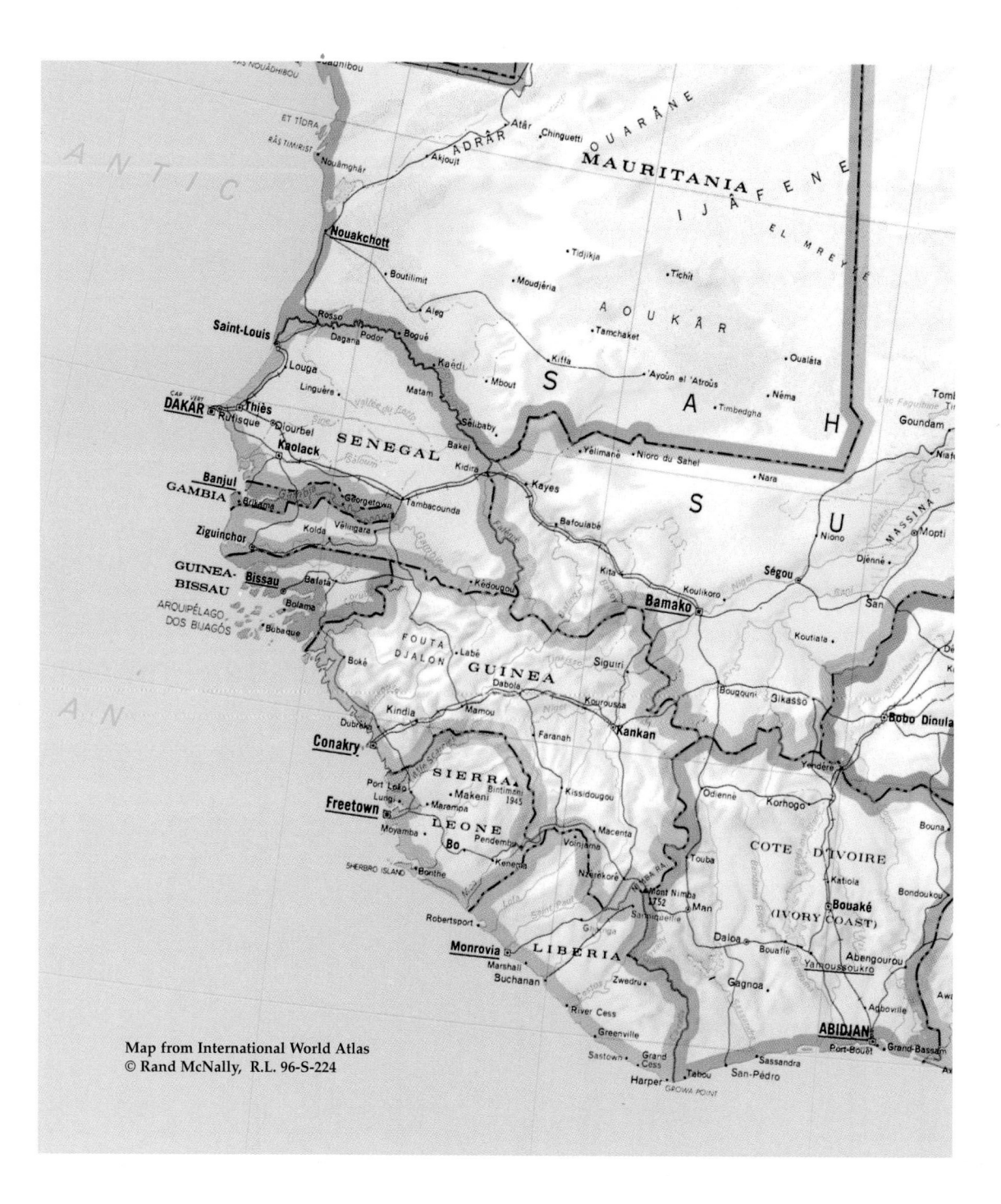

Map from International World Atlas
© Rand McNally, R.L. 96-S-224

Enchantment of the World

SENEGAL

by Margaret Beaton

Consultant for Senegal: Mamadou Chef Guèye, M.A., Sidwell
Friends High School, Washington, D.C.; President and Founder,
La Francophonie, Ltd.

CHILDREN'S PRESS®
A Division of Grolier Publishing
New York • London • Hong Kong • Sydney
Danbury, Connecticut

Peul mothers, wearing traditional clothing, proudly show off their children.

Project Editor and Design:
Jean Blashfield Black

**Library of Congress
Cataloging-in-Publication Data**

Beaton, Margaret.
  Senegal / by Margaret Beaton.
    p. cm. -- (Enchantment of the world)
  Includes index.
  Summary: Describes the geography, history, cul-
ture, religion, and people of the African nation of
Senegal.
  ISBN 0-516-20304-5
  1. Senegal--Juvenile literature. [1. Senegal.] I.
Title. II. Series.
DT549.22.B43   1997
916.63--dc21   96-51578
                                                      CIP
                                                       AC

Photo credits ©: Art Resource: 35, 41
(Giraudon); Asia Access: 18, 23, 58, 67, 75, 81,
91 right (Naomi Duguid); Charlotte Kahler:
72, 74 left, 76 left; Corbis-Bettmann: 39 left, 44
bottom, 111 left; David Johnson: 5, 12, 16, 19
left, 33, 54, 56 left, 61 left, 71, 73, 76 right, 86,
89, 91 left, 93 right, 94, 96, 100 left, 101, 102
top, 106, 107, 111 right; Gamma-Liaison: 84
(Agostini); Impact Visuals: 4, 70 (Catherine
Smith); Jason Lauré: 6, 8, 15, 19 right, 65, 74
left, 83, 93 left, 95, 100 right; Joan Iaconetti:
cover, 10, 21, 27, 50, 52, 61 right, 66 left, 68, 79
left, 92 left, 98; Library of Congress: 39 right;
North Wind Picture Archives: 30, 31, 36; Panos
Pictures: 88 (Ron Giling), 59, 102 bottom, 108
right (Jeremy Hartley), 20 (Bruce Pator), 64
(Chris Sattlberger); Photri: 9, 53, 56 right, 79,
80; Publiphoto: 85 (Paul G. Adam); United
Nations: 92 right; UPI/Corbis-Bettmann: 37,
44 top, 47, 49, 104 left; Valan Photos: 25, 60, 63
(Christine Osborne), 66 right (Val & Alan
Wilkinson); Wolfgang Kaehler: 11, 13, 17, 24,
28, 38, 43, 55, 57, 104 right, 108 left, 109.

Cover photo: A fishing village in the
Casamance region of Senegal

This is one of many food shops in the Sandanga Market of Dakar.

TABLE OF CONTENTS

A griot, or storyteller, relates the history of a village in Senegal to fascinated listeners. Much of Senegal's history is known only through such storytelling.

Chapter 1

STORIES OF SENEGAL

In a small village on a dusty savanna, an old man sits under the scant shade of a gnarled baobab tree. The sun is hot and no wind is blowing. It is afternoon, and people have slowed to avoid the heat. A bird cries in the distance, but no one pays attention.

Seated on the ground around the man are about twenty people—small children, a few teenagers, women with babies, and some old people. They are listening in rapt attention to what the man is saying. The man is a *griot*, a combination storyteller, musician, historian, and wandering minstrel. He knows all the stories of Senegal's rich past—of the great Ghana and Mali Empires, of gold and wealth, of kings and slaves and religious leaders called *marabouts*, of Wolof warriors and national heroes of revolution and independence. He also knows ancient myths about owls and ants, about spirits that inhabit the wind, and about the forces of life and death.

Today he is telling a story that involves the villagers personally, the story of a battle that took place many years ago. He relates all the details, making the story come alive by acting out parts. He names the listeners' ancestors who took part in the battle—who won and who lost. This is not just any story they are hearing—it is the history of families of the village.

The griot knows the complex family relationships of everyone. He helps them understand and remember who they are, where

Senegal varies greatly from north to south. The northern part of the country overlaps the Sahara Desert, where nomads move their herds across great sandy plains.

they belong, and why. He helps them understand their loyalties and obligations, what duties they must perform, and who will help them. He gives them a strong sense of identity—and with it a feeling of peace and serenity that is often the envy of Westerners.

The story of Senegal is told across the countryside in a thousand ways, among the peoples known as the Wolof, the Serer, the Mandinka, and the Tukulor.

Meanwhile, many miles away in the capital, Dakar, other Senegalese work as computer programmers or bankers in modern skyscrapers that loom over the white sand beaches lining the Atlantic Ocean. They read newspapers in French or Wolof to find out the news of the day, as well as books to discover their history.

In the melting pot of Dakar, many people say they don't even know if their ancestors were Wolof, Peul, or Mandinka. Yet in the evening they may go to clubs and theaters to hear professional griots sing and play the songs and tell the stories of Senegal. Perhaps they wish to recover some of the peace and serenity that comes from being in touch with a unique past.

Dakar, the capital, is a colorful mix of modern buildings, traditional dress, and tropical greenery. Shown in the inset is a modern government office building in Dakar.

The weaverbirds of Senegal weave spherical nests that they hang in large communities from the fronds of palm trees.

Chapter 2

JUST BELOW
THE SAHARA

Senegal is located on the Atlantic Ocean in the northwest corner of the part of Africa that is below the Sahara Desert, called the sub-Sahara. Mauritania is to the north, Mali to the east, Guinea to the southeast, and Guinea-Bissau to the south. The country of The Gambia cuts through the heart of Senegal's territory along the Gambia River for 200 miles (320 kilometers). The northern and central areas of Senegal are dry. Moving south, the dryness gradually gives way to swamps in the far southwest and tropical forests in the southeast.

The northern part of Senegal is on the lower edge of the great Sahara Desert. This desert ecosystem spans the entire width of North Africa, from Senegal on the Atlantic Coast to Ethiopia on the east. The lower Sahara, sometimes called the Sahel Desert, has

A separate nation called The Gambia lies in the heart of Senegal, along both sides of the Gambia River. The entire region, including The Gambia and Senegal, is often called Senegambia. Shown is a fishing village on the Gambia River.

Some areas of Senegal that were previously farmlands have been turned into desert, where cattle such as these find only scrub plants to eat.

more rainfall than the main part of the Sahara. There is enough rainfall for various scrubby grasses to grow, and even for animals to be grazed. But rain falls only occasionally and is not predictable. Droughts are common. In recent times, droughts have been long and severe, turning more and more grassland into desert. The nomads—people who wander from place to place to find pasture-land—have been forced to move farther and farther south.

Going south through Senegal, the dry scrubby desert land in the north becomes gradually more humid. With more rainfall, there are more farmers and fewer nomads. Moisture increases until eventually mangrove swamps or tropical rain forests appear. Traveling through Senegal one goes from a sub-Saharan desert to a tropical jungle—seeing camels in the north, monkeys and crocodiles in the south, and a great deal in between.

There also is a change in the people. Some of the people in the north are lighter-skinned Arabic-speaking people, or Berbers, related to the Moors of Mauritania and southern Morocco. They wear long, loose robes to protect their bodies from sun and sand.

The Senegal River, which forms part of the northern border, is a green area of fishing villages (above). Nomadic Muslims follow Islamic law, as well as find comfort in the sun, by wearing long, light-colored robes (right).

Farther south, the people have darker skin, and they wear very few clothes because of the heat and humidity. They want to expose their skin to let perspiration escape, keeping them cool. Men wear only shorts, which is practical in the tropical climate.

People in the north wear long robes also because they are Muslims, followers of Islam, and Islamic law requires bodies to be covered. Northern Senegalese people live close to Arabic Islamic countries, and have been influenced by them more than the people of the south have. Some people in southern Senegal have resisted both Islam and Christianity and kept their native religions.

GEOGRAPHY AND HISTORY

Senegal's geography has played a key role in shaping its customs and its history. Senegal is close to Arabic countries, but it is also closer to Europe than any other sub-Saharan country—and closer to the Americas, too. These factors have influenced Senegal's development.

It was natural for the Senegalese to trade with Arabs. The Berbers who traveled the trade routes across the Sahara exchanged their salt for African gold. They also brought information, knowledge, and eventually, their religion, Islam, to Senegal.

As the Berbers traded with Europeans, they told tales of the plentiful gold in Africa's interior (in present-day Mali). This eventually led Europeans to travel into Africa in pursuit of it. They came down the coast in ships, and often landed at the first harbors they could find—Saint-Louis and Dakar. There, the Europeans began to trade with the Africans from the interior.

Senegal's coastline juts farther out into the Atlantic Ocean than any other point in Africa. Dakar, the capital, is on the tip of the peninsula in the Atlantic. Gorée Island, to the west of Dakar, became a secure port from which valuable cargoes of slaves were shipped to the Americas.

Because of its nearness to Europe, Dakar was a natural choice as the capital of France's nineteenth-century West African colonial empire, which included the present-day countries of Benin, Guinea, Mali, Ivory Coast, Mauritania, Niger, Burkina Faso, and, of course, Senegal. (Guinea-Bissau was Portuguese.) Dakar was very important, and is still the most influential city in West Africa.

LAND AND CLIMATE

Senegal is quite close to the equator, so it is always warm, even in winter. There are really only two distinct seasons in Senegal.

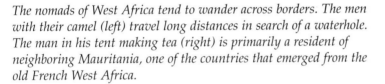

The nomads of West Africa tend to wander across borders. The men with their camel (left) travel long distances in search of a waterhole. The man in his tent making tea (right) is primarily a resident of neighboring Mauritania, one of the countries that emerged from the old French West Africa.

Winter, or the dry season, lasts from November to June and is very dry. June brings abundant summer rains when almost all planting takes place. The rest of summer, or the rainy season, becomes hot and humid.

The coolest part of Senegal is in the high elevations of the foothills of the Fouta Djallon mountain range, most of which actually lies across the border in Guinea. Except for these foothills, Senegal is mostly very flat. As a result, the rivers are slow moving and collect a great deal of silt. They often branch out into many rambling tributaries, and along the coast their estuaries produce very marshy and swampy areas.

Several important rivers flow through Senegal—the Senegal River (which forms the northern border with Mauritania), the

A man from the Thiès region demonstrates how dry the soil in this arid region can become during the dry season.

Saloum, the Gambia, and the Casamance. In a semiarid land, these rivers provide an extremely important source of water. As rivers flood their banks in rainy seasons, they leave behind fertile soil. People can raise crops here part of the year, and can eat the fish year-round. However, the lower reaches of these rivers dry up in the hot seasons, forcing some people to become nomads.

RIVERS, DESERTS, AND JUNGLES

The Senegal River serves as a northern border separating Senegal from Mauritania. The river originates in the mountains outside Senegal's border, flows northwest, cutting through the Sahel Desert, and then empties into the Atlantic Ocean at Saint-Louis.

The land bordering the Senegal River is fertile. But this is the Sahel Desert, and away from the river's edge, the land is quite arid, with rocky, sandy soil. There is enough seasonal rain, however, for certain sturdy grasses, small bushes, desert date trees, and different kinds of acacia trees. The acacia trees yield gum arabic, which is sold for use in candles and medicines. The grasses

These nomadic women are fortunate to have found an area in the Ferlo with plenty of fresh grasses.

provide food for the cattle that are herded here. The people who live in these areas are nomads who keep cattle and goats, which graze on the sparse grasses.

The grasses are easily depleted, and the nomads must move constantly to find fresh pasture for their animals. The nomadic people who live in this area also live in Mauritania. They travel back and forth between Senegal and Mauritania in search of pasture, and to engage in trade. Overgrazing and the stripping of trees for firewood have injured the delicate ecology of the area and contributed to the droughts.

In stark contrast to the rocky desert, the valley of the Senegal River is a green and fertile strip from 10 to 25 miles (16 to 40 kilometers) wide. Like the Nile River in Egypt, the Senegal River floods its banks once a year and leaves behind fertile soil, silt, and moisture needed for growing crops.

When the river floods, it covers the entire valley. The Tukulor

Passengers and some cargo can travel in this long boat on the Senegal River, which extends from the city of Saint-Louis into the mountains of Mali.

and Peul people who live in the valley build their homes on high ground or on stilts in anticipation of the floods. When the rains stop, the water begins to evaporate and the river recedes, leaving a wet, fertile coating of soil. The people quickly plant their seeds (primarily millet and groundnuts, or peanuts). They harvest the crops in a few months and live off them until the next year's rain, when they plant again. The Peul return to grazing their cattle, moving ever southward to find water and grasses for their cattle as vegetation dries up. Fish are plentiful year-round, except where the river dries up completely.

The Vallée du Ferlo River is a large tributary of the Senegal River that runs for a while just south of it. The entire area around the Vallée du Ferlo and the Senegal Rivers is also called the Ferlo. It is a sandy savanna where nomads graze their cattle. It is very dry and isolated. A few lakes in the north of the Ferlo provide

A Peul, or Fulani, home in the Ferlo (above) may be left behind when crops fail and the people become nomadic. Savannas may be dotted with huge baobab trees, seen at the right in an area where warthogs roam.

some fishing and water for agriculture, but it is one of the poorest regions. The nomadic Peul (also called the Fulani) live here.

The western part of the Ferlo Desert becomes more and more fertile closer to the Atlantic Coast. The area around the cities of Diourbel, Kaolack, and Thiès is a key agricultural area. Although the sandy soil dries up completely after the rainy season, it is highly productive when it is fertile.

The Falémé River serves as the eastern border between Senegal and Mali. It originates in the mountains and flows south and then north to meet the Senegal River. The area around it is poor savanna, or grassland, with only tough baobab trees and some acacia trees and grasses. Closer to the mountains in the south, however, tall and tough teak and mahogany trees start to appear.

In the south, the equatorial climate and humidity produce lush

Some parts of Senegal, especially in the south, are wet enough to support tropical rain forest.

growths of bamboo and trees that shelter a great variety of animals. The great Niokolo Koba National Park protects elephants, leopards, antelope, hyenas, wild dogs, jackals, hippopotamuses, water buffaloes, crocodiles, monkeys, chimpanzees, porcupines, and birds. Over three million birds come to the park at various times, including storks and herons. Lions are not as plentiful in Senegal as they are elsewhere in Africa, but the subspecies of lion native to this area is the largest in Africa.

Several ethnic groups live outside the park: the Diallonke, a Guinean people, inhabit the foothills of the Fouta Djallon mountains and the Peul stay in low-lying areas.

THE COASTS

Most of Senegal's people live along the Atlantic Coast where ports support trading activities and business opportunities. They

Huge, old, and tough termite mounds are found among the palm trees of some coastal areas.

also can count on an abundance of ocean fish to eat and to sell, and a fertile growing area around the rivers that empty into the ocean.

Life here is very pleasant. The coastal area benefits from cool breezes that blow in from the Atlantic Ocean all year round. The ocean current that passes along the west coast of Africa comes from the north, so the water is quite cold, cooling the air that blows across the water.

The long coast of Senegal has its own special ecology, a "belt" of dunes, swamps, lagoons, and estuaries. This belt is about 15 to 20 miles (24 to 32 kilometers) wide in the north, narrowing toward the south. Because much of the water that soaks the land is salt-water, it is not good for most crops. The mangrove-filled saltwater marshes provide excellent fishing, however. Intensive fishing is practiced in the ocean as well as the rivers and estuaries. Birds and wildlife are abundant in many areas.

The Senegalese call the coast from Saint-Louis to Dakar *La Grande Côte*, meaning "the Long Coast," and the coast from Dakar to the Sine-Saloum Rivers is *La Petite Côte*, or "the Short Coast." Saint-Louis is at the top of the Grande Côte, at the border with Mauritania. It originated on an island where the Senegal River empties into the Atlantic Ocean, and then grew to include an area on the mainland as it became an important center for trade on routes to Europe and all points south by ocean.

The relationship between the Senegal River and the Atlantic Ocean is rather special here. During the dry season, water evaporates and the Senegal River shrinks. Because the land is so flat, the ocean tides flow a long way into the river. During the dry season, the estuary, or mouth, of the Senegal River is often full of saltwater for almost 300 miles (483 kilometers) inland.

The combination of salty and freshwater, and the various plants and insects that live in marshy areas, attract an astounding number and variety of migratory birds and waterfowl. There is an important bird sanctuary in the estuary, the *Oiseaux du Djoudj* (Birds of Djoudj) National Park. It is the third most important bird sanctuary in the world, protecting more than three million birds of many kinds at various times. A peak time for migratory waterfowl is in winter. Tourists come from all over to see ducks, pelicans, spoonbills, storks, and the thousands of pink flamingos that feed on the shrimp and shellfish.

On a long secluded peninsula of white sand-dune beach just south of Saint-Louis is another protected reserve, the *Langue de Barbarie* (Barbary Tongue) National Park. It is internationally important because rare sea turtles nest there.

The valuable silt deposited in the delta region at Saint-Louis is

Pelicans flock among the marsh grasses that grow in the mixture of freshwater and saltwater found in the Oiseaux du Djoudj National Park.

quite fertile and produces significant quantities of rice, vegetables, and sugarcane. However, there is so much silt in the mouth of the river that large ocean-going vessels can no longer dock here.

Fishing villages dot the rest of the Grande Côte. Expert Yoff fishermen walk out into the ocean with their huge nets or go out to the rough sea in *pirogues,* canoes dug out of tree trunks.

The Cap Vert Peninsula is the most distinctive feature on the map. It extends farther out into the Atlantic Ocean than any point in Africa. Dakar is at the tip. The whole peninsula is densely populated, with many suburbs and satellite towns extending in all directions from Dakar.

The Petite Côte south of Dakar enjoys a pleasant climate, with palm trees and beaches and steep cliffs of red rock. With cool trade winds, sunshine, and nearness to Dakar, it has become an important resort area for tourists from Europe. The resorts are

The Atlantic beaches serve as a town square for this busy fishing village south of Dakar.

interspersed with fishing villages, extending south along the coast past Gambia to the Casamance region and the border with Guinea-Bissau.

Both natives and tourists fish for swordfish, tuna, marlin, sea bass, sailfish, barracuda, and sharks. Dolphin also are found in these waters.

The two primary ethnic groups of the Petite Côte are the Serer and the Lebou people. While over 90 percent of Senegalese are Muslims, the 5 percent who are Christian are concentrated along the Petite Côte. The French influence is still strong. In the nineteenth century, the French opened several schools here, offering free education to all Senegalese.

South of the Petite Côte, the Sine and Saloum Rivers flow into the ocean. The Sine-Saloum region includes both the coast and the inland areas along the rivers. The coastline from here south is markedly different from the Grande and Petite Côtes to the north.

The rivers of the Petite Côte support abundant wildlife, including many crocodiles.

It becomes more watery and humid, covered with small creeks and marshes. While not very comfortable, the area supports abundant wildlife, fresh- and saltwater fish and shellfish, birds such as egrets and cormorants, three kinds of crocodiles (the pygmy, bottlenose, and great Nile), as well as hippopotamuses and manatees.

Rainfall is ample in much of the Sine-Saloum, and so is vegetation, which supports monkeys, small forest deer, and even some baboons. But despite its greater rainfall, the lower reaches of the Saloum River eventually dry up in summer, too. The eastern region is as dry as the desert of the north and center.

THE GAMBIA

Surrounded on three sides by Senegal is another country, The Gambia, which lies along the Gambia River. In colonial times,

France claimed the Senegal area, and England claimed the Gambia River area. When these countries became independent of foreign powers, The Gambia became a separate country. Gambians have strong cultural and commercial ties to Britain, and English is their official language.

A few of Senegal's ethnic groups live also in The Gambia, but not many. Relations between The Gambia and Senegal are friendly, and they trade with each other and easily cross each other's borders.

The Gambia does not encompass the entire Gambia River, part of which flows in Senegal, too. The narrower, eastern portion of the Gambia River is in Senegal, in an area referred to as the Upper Gambia. Senegal's Niokolo Koba National Park, which has a marvelous variety of wildlife, is in this area.

CASAMANCE

South of The Gambia, moisture increases further, and the air becomes distinctly humid. Vegetation is very dense along the coast, thick with mangroves, oil palms, and raffia palms. At the heart of this coastal region is the Casamance River. Its many tributaries contain perch, catfish, oysters, crabs, and crawfish; geese and ducks make their homes here, too. Near the coast, both the river and the rainy climate create excellent conditions for abundant cultivation of rice, millet, sorghum, maize (corn), groundnuts, dates and other fruit, cotton, and palm oil. But once again, away from the coast this becomes a dryer area.

The Casamance is home to the Diola, Mandinka, and Tukulor people. They live fairly isolated from the rest of Senegal and from foreign influences. One reason is the lack of a railway linking the

This fishing village in the Casamance region south of The Gambia is typical of many Senegalese fishing villages. The people of the Casamance would like to form their own country.

area to other regions, limiting both trade and interaction. These people trade not so much with other Senegalese as with their neighbors in Guinea-Bissau. They have resisted both Islam and Christianity, and most still practice their traditional animistic religions, believing there are spirits in all living things.

The woodland peoples that inhabit the forests to the east are even more isolated. They are very shy and avoid contact with people not of their own tribe.

On the Casamance coast, this isolation has resulted in some unique tourist villages. Typical Diola villages and huts were constructed on the coast so that tourists can experience rustic African life in a controlled environment, and they are very popular.

Two very different views in Senegal's history: the holding of captives for sale into slavery, seen above in a re-enactment on Gorée Island; and the new Parliament Building in Dakar (below), where democratic procedure reigns.

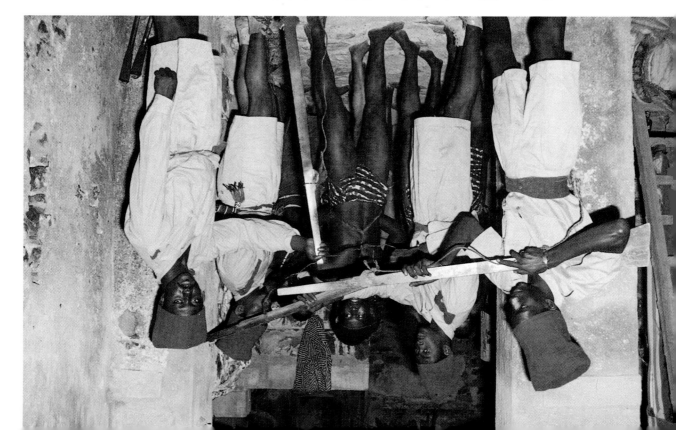

Chapter 3

ANCIENT EMPIRES TO INDEPENDENCE

Much of the early history of Senegal has been lost, because there was no written language to record great events. Information and history were transmitted from generation to generation in the form of stories. Other countries that did have written language had no contact with sub-Saharan Africa. The great Sahara Desert and the tropical jungles kept travelers out.

Historians have been able to piece together the early history based on a combination of brief accounts written by ancient Greek, Roman, and Arab traders and the stories that Africans themselves told, as well as by examining the physical evidence.

In the time of the initial European exploration in the fifteenth century, and then in the colonial period that followed, Europeans recorded observations and events from their own perspective. Gradually, the Senegalese acquired education, but many, influenced by European values, did not appreciate their own culture. Only in the twentieth century has there been an African view of African history. And it is still evolving.

The history of Senegal is closely entwined with the history of the whole West African region. It's a shared history that includes Mali, The Gambia, Mauritania, and the French and Portuguese.

EARLY HISTORY

People have been living in the Senegal area for 15,000 years. The archeological evidence used to determine this is based on Paleolithic axes and Neolithic two-headed axes. The land was dramatically different then. The borders of the Sahara Desert were far to the north. Senegal was very fertile, with a great deal of plant and animal life, especially around the rivers. The destruction of fertile land by the southward expansion of the Sahara has been going on for centuries, but it has been gradual—not with the alarming speed of the last fifty years.

Around 800 B.C., the nomadic tribes that inhabited the region started to establish permanent settlements. These hunters and gatherers worshiped gods of the natural world—the sun, moon, panthers, crocodiles, snakes, gods that inhabited trees and rivers, and gold, which was fairly abundant in West Africa.

In 500 B.C., Hanno the Great, a navigator living in Tunis on the Mediterranean Sea, traveled to West Africa. He wrote of many things, including elephants and hippopotamuses. Inspired, another Mediterranean sailor, Euthymenes, came and took notes, and then in 470 B.C., a Persian came in to map the area. The

The Greek historian Herodotus

Caravans of trade goods came from the north into Senegal.

Greek historian Herodotus wrote more extensively of the area, noting that the people made a wine from palm trees, which they still do today.

Their curiosity satisfied, and with other things to occupy them, foreigners ceased exploration for several hundred years, until about 140 B.C. A Greek named Polybius visited the Senegal coast and wrote about it in more detail. He noted large, prosperous, civilized settlements in the Senegal and Gambia regions and farther into the interior around the Niger River in Mali. The inhabitants were trading extensively with each other, in gold, salt, iron, copper, and Phoenician glass beads brought by the Arab traders via the Sahara. He also noted that slaves were taken from along the rivers and traded to people from the Sahara and the north. This would not have shocked Polybius, because slavery also was practiced in Greece and Rome.

By A.D. 141, the Romans ruled northern Africa, and used camels to travel across the Sahara and beyond. They drew the first known map of the Senegal area. When the great geographer Ptolemy created maps of the world as it was then known, Senegal was included, with the Senegal and Gambia Rivers, and even a settlement on the Senegal River called Magiora.

Historians also have found that Phoenician and even Viking sailors knew the area well enough to have charts of it. However, they had no significant contacts with the cultures, and no influences in either direction. While travel through the desert was easy by camel, the dense foliage, tropical heat, and diseases common to the interior were extremely forbidding. Exploration was mostly limited to the coastal region.

Nomadic Berber people of the Sahara traveled widely. A branch of Berbers called Zenega began to migrate into the north of Senegal. It may be the Zenega who gave the Senegal River its name. Then the area to the south also came to be called Senegal.

AFRICAN EMPIRES

Around the end of the third century, one West African tribe began to grow in power and strength over the others, spreading out to dominate the entire area. Today, Ghana is a small country southeast of Senegal on the Gulf of Guinea. But in those times, tribes related to modern-day Ghanaians inhabited an area around present-day Mali, a vital trading crossroads for Arabs and Africans. Iron was found along the Ghana River, and the Ghanaians learned the art of metal smelting, probably from the Arabs with whom they traded. This created an important "Iron Age" that enabled other advances to occur. The Ghanaians expanded to dominate the Zenega in the north of Senegal and the Wolof and Serer peoples in the south.

There was one king of the Ghana empire, with other, lesser kings paying tribute to him. The wealth of his empire was so

The religion of Islam spread to Senegal very early, and today 90 percent of the people are Muslim. These Muslim men are gathered for prayer at a country mosque.

impressive that Arab traders described the king of Ghana as "the richest man in the world."

Although the Ghana Empire continued to the tenth century, the Tukulor people began to dominate in the Senegal River Valley around the ninth and tenth centuries.

In the eleventh century, the religion of Islam came to Senegal. It had begun in Saudi Arabia in the A.D. 600s, and spread quickly in all directions, mainly along Arab desert and trading routes. It was spread "by word and by sword," as conquering armies imposed their religion on conquered people. The Almoravids, a branch of Muslims, brought their armies into Senegal in the eleventh century, and the Ghana Empire fought back. Eventually, however, the people of the Ghana Empire and the Tukulor were conquered and converted to Islam. Some ethnic groups of southern Senegal, however, tended to resist Islam, even after they were conquered. These people established the Songhai Empire that controlled The Gambia and Fouta Djallon mountains for a brief time.

By the fourteenth century, the Mandinka people, who had been subjects of the Ghanaians, had become strong enough to rebel and create their own empire, the Mali Empire. They converted to Islam and conquered and converted the Wolof, Tukulor, and, with some difficulty, the Serer. The Mali Empire was twice as large as the Ghana Empire. Living in the most fertile areas, the Malis also possessed great wealth in iron, copper, and gold, and traded extensively with the Arabs. Their civilization was very advanced, and their wealth was legendary. Fourteenth-century maps of the area were illustrated with images of African kings on ornate thrones surrounded by riches.

As with the Ghana Empire, local groups and small kingdoms had the right to rule themselves but paid tribute to the Mali kings. However, as these ethnic groups gradually became Islamic, they became unified in a way that enabled more trade and significant exchanges of ideas with the Arab countries of the north.

EUROPEAN EXPLORATION

Arab traders carried to Europeans tales of gold to be found in the African interior. Europe had just started to use gold as a standard of exchange, and the rare metal was in great demand. In the 1400s, all of Europe sought both gold and spices, and the great Age of Exploration began. Marco Polo had traveled to China bringing back spices and silk. Christopher Columbus reported on the existence of the "New World," and Magellan sailed around South America and across the Pacific. Tales of gold made European explorers ignore the dangers to be met in the jungles of the West African interior.

A fifteenth-century European map of the discoveries of West Africa shows, at the bottom, left of center, the king of Senegal holding a golden orb.

The first of these explorers to reach the Senegal area was a Portuguese navigator, Nuno Tristão. In 1443 he sailed up the mouth of the Senegal River. Later Portuguese sailed farther up the river to the interior and were awed by the gold jewelry the Africans wore so casually. They were also impressed by the abundance of cotton and rice.

In 1465 the Portuguese traded goods with a local Gambia River chief in exchange for his gold and his slaves. The Europeans observed that a kind of caste system was well established among the tribes in West Africa. *Caste,* a Portuguese word, means "family," "strain," or "race." In a caste system, people are born into a set social division, generally based on occupation, heritage, wealth, or religion. It was extremely difficult, if not impossible, to

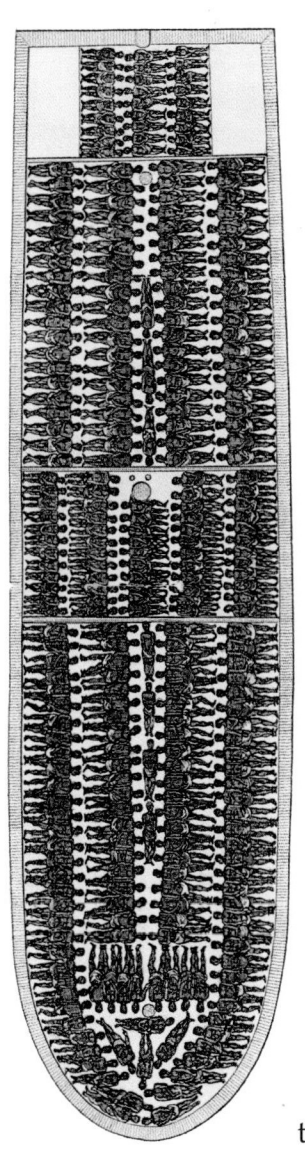

An old French drawing shows the most efficient way to pack captive slaves into a ship for transport to the New World. Less than half of them survive the journey.

rise above the caste into which one was born. The caste system in West Africa included a slave caste.

In pursuit of their share of riches, French explorers came in 1570, followed by the English and the Dutch. Europeans who explored and traded in Africa began to name the coastal areas for the main export—the Gold Coast, the Grain Coast, the Ivory Coast, and the Gum (meaning gum arabic) Coast. The Senegambia region was called the Slave Coast.

THE SLAVE TRADE

From about 1500 to 1810, perhaps as many as 200 million Africans were taken from Africa to be sold to slave traders to work on plantations in the Caribbean and in North and South America. Some were abducted by slave traders. More often, though, they were sold by the local African kings, to whom slavery was an established institution. The slaves were either captives taken prisoner in battle or they were born into the caste of slaves used for labor, members of which were often bought and sold. Slavery was also occasionally used as punishment for crimes.

The slave trade was extremely profitable for many. The African kings used the money they acquired to buy guns to fight their enemies. The plantation owners in the New World grew rich from

In the TV series based on Alex Haley's novel Roots, *Kunta Kinte, played by LeVar Burton (right), was taken prisoner in The Gambia.*

the labor of their slaves. The Europeans and Arabs made a profit from the trade. The slave trade continued until there were enough slaves in the New World, then it died down.

A majority of the slaves were taken from the Gambia area. Alex Haley's epic novel *Roots* set the hero, Kunta Kinte, in a village of The Gambia among the Mandinka people. But slavers also took slaves from the western area inland to Nigeria and down the coast.

Slave-holding compounds began to spring up all along the Senegambia coast, where slaves were taken to await boats to carry them to the Americas. The compounds were often island fortresses that could be protected from pirates. Escape was almost impossible. The main slave-trading posts in Senegambia were at Saint-Louis, Gorée Island, Rufisque, Portudal, Joal, Albreda, James Island, and Juffure (mentioned in Alex Haley's *Roots)*, as well as on the Senegal River, at Podor, Matam, and Bakel.

Initially, relations between the African kings and Europeans were friendly because both sides benefited from the trade. Occasionally there was armed conflict, but conflict within and between ethnic groups was normal. Wolof fought against Tukulor

Gorée Island was the earliest settlement in Senegal. It became the center of the slave trade.

and often against other Wolof subgroups. The Senegalese accepted the Europeans as just another group to deal with. But as more and more French came, the African kings began to be concerned that the French would take over completely.

In the late 1600s, Muslim leaders tried to rebel against black slave-trading aristocracies. The rebellion was soon put down with European guns. The African kings then realized the value of an arsenal of guns to defend their territories and keep their power. To buy guns from Europeans, they had to sell something. So they sold more and more slaves to get more and more guns to defend themselves from the ever-growing number of European intruders.

EUROPEANS SETTLE

The Dutch were the first Europeans to establish a permanent trading settlement in Senegal, in 1617 on Gorée Island. The French soon followed, with a trading station at Saint-Louis in 1621, then a fort also at Saint-Louis. In 1633 France authorized the formation of

Botanist Michel Adanson

Burning the throne in 1848 was one way the French public made the king keep his promise of equality and a constitutional government.

an official Senegal trading company with a monopoly for all trade in that area. In 1661 the English chartered an English trading company. More trading settlements appeared along the coast and near the rivers. The French came to dominate the Senegal region, and the English eventually settled along the Gambia River.

In addition to slaves, trade in gum, gold, and iron increased. The continuing tales of gold found deep in the interior attracted more European explorers. Not all were motivated by love of gold, however. Some were motivated by love of science. Michel Adanson, a French botanist, explored the Senegal interior for five years, and in 1757 published his *Natural History of Senegal.* The French introduced cotton-growing to the Saint-Louis area, as well as groundnuts, which would eventually become the most important crop for sustenance and export, mainly as peanut oil.

Some explorers became obsessed with finding the sources of the major rivers. But it wasn't until 1818 that Gaspard-Theodore Mollien was able to cross the Ferlo and discover the sources of the Senegal and Gambia Rivers in the Fouta Djallon mountains.

The end of the eighteenth century signaled a new period in world history. After the Revolutionary War in America (1775-1783) and the French Revolution (1789-1799), ideas of freedom and equality spread throughout the world. Although slavery was later reintroduced by Napoleon, it was condemned in France immediately after the revolution. It took a while for these ideas of equality to penetrate to Africa and previously isolated countries.

Britain decided in 1807 to prohibit all British citizens from engaging in slavery. They extended the law to all their territories, which included part of The Gambia. France abolished the slave trade in 1818, but it did not prohibit slavery in its territories until 1848. During this period, France underwent tumultuous changes at home. Following the French Revolution, a conservative regime ruled France after 1830. They withdrew many of the rights and privileges the revolution had granted. Then in 1848, the Second Republic was created, and the generous ideals of freedom and equality were restored. Among other things, the Second Republic government extended many basic human rights to people born in parts of its colonies. Those people, black or white, born in four coastal cities in Senegal were given full French citizenship.

A FRENCH COLONY

Love of freedom and equality aside, however, France was not about to give up its profitable colonial empire. It held its colonies with an iron fist, and tried to expand their territories. The French used force, but because they were always outnumbered, they also kept control by playing one local ethnic group against the others. The French used the long history of ethnic rivalry to "divide and conquer." They did this in a way that would keep the groups unable to unite against France. France practiced favoritism and

Louis Faidherbe was governor for only ten years, but during that time he laid the foundations for Senegal's future and the way the Senegalese would be treated in a French Empire.

encouraged dissension among the different ethnic groups.

Eventually, the conflicts the French encouraged became counter-productive, so they switched to a policy of pacifying the warring peoples. The merchant settlers were particularly unhappy with the instability and asked that General Louis Faidherbe be appointed governor in 1854. He was very popular for having fought effectively against the armies of Al Haj Omar, a religious leader in the north.

Under Faidherbe's progressive rule, Senegal made great strides forward on a human and practical level. Faidherbe established free schools for Senegalese children and scholarships that sent them to school in France. He also provided health services to the African people and established a newspaper. He began promoting the export of groundnuts for export, and was responsible for the first metal bridge built at Saint-Louis.

Most of all, he respected the "native populations," which was far from the case for other Europeans in most African countries. Europeans assumed the "native populations" were hopelessly primitive, if not barbarian; good only to be used as laborers or servants. Faidherbe allowed the Senegalese access to French civilization and left them free to develop. For Faidherbe, to be

French was a state of mind, not of birth. However, as intellectual Senegalese were encouraged to acquire French culture, they had to reject their own. Faidherbe and the liberal French did not appreciate African culture in any way. It wasn't until much later that the Senegalese had the option of combining the two cultures.

Although many Senegalese had been Muslim for centuries, they were either a minority or not very enthusiastic in practicing Islam. Starting in the nineteenth century, however, people began to turn to Islam in record numbers. Senegalese Islamic leaders began to be politically more powerful than the local kings, and there were even wars between the rival Muslim brotherhoods, which were closely knit subgroups of Muslims.

By the mid-1800s, Al Haj Omar, a Tukulor Muslim, started a *jihad*, or "holy war," against irreligious Senegalese and against France. Although he lost to the French army, he won a war of ideas. The Senegalese became passionate Muslims. The Islam they practiced would serve as a unifying force, a rallying point to rebel against the French throughout the remainder of the nineteenth century. The armed rebellions ended in 1895 when Lat Dior, the last of the Wolof kings, was defeated and killed.

FRENCH WEST AFRICA

In the nineteenth century, European countries competed for control of the natural resources of the new colonies. France had been defeated in the Americas, so they looked to Africa. Toward the end of the 1800s, they had targeted the whole area from the Atlantic Coast to the Nile River for takeover. With great effort and daring (and bloodshed), the French West African Empire was

The waterfront of Saint-Louis is lined with French colonial buildings.

established. By 1895, the boundaries of Senegal were set as a part of French West Africa, an official federation of the French colonies. The area south and east of Senegal was named the French Sudan, the area north of the Senegal River was called Mauritania. These territories remained the same until 1958.

By 1900, internal warfare had ended. The warring ethnic groups were subdued, and the resulting stability cleared the way for even greater development by the French. Railways crisscrossed the empire, facilitating development at all levels. Groundnuts, maize, and *manioc* (cassava) crops were well established and abundant.

Among the French territories, Senegal was the only one where certain native Senegalese could have French citizenship and elect representatives. The residents of the four cities of Saint-Louis, Gorée, Rufisque, and Dakar, called communes, had full citizenship and could elect representatives to self-governing municipal councils—and even to the French parliament itself. Blaise Diagne was the first Senegalese (and the first African) to be elected to France's National Assembly, in 1914.

French leaders who played roles in World War II Senegal: Marshal Pétain (above) and Charles de Gaulle (below)

By 1920, the General Council that governed Senegal had eight white and thirty-two black members. It was the only multiracial legislative body in Africa. The Senegalese were aware of their special position in the French world and in the black African world. The elite strove to be even more integrated into the French Empire. The education they received from the French enabled them to achieve wealth and prominence.

Not surprisingly, there was tension between the educated Senegalese of the communes and the uneducated Senegalese who lived elsewhere. There were actually two official classes of people in Senegal: the "citizens" who had voting and other rights, and the "subjects," who did not. The citizens were required to renounce traditional laws in favor of French laws. The subjects kept traditional laws, such as those regarding marriage, but could not vote.

One of these citizens, Léopold Sédar Senghor, was sent to study at a university in France in the 1920s. Although he loved French culture, he became homesick and began to appreciate African culture. He met other Africans, such as the black Caribbean-born poet, Aimé Césaire. They reflected on what it means to be African and why it is special. For the first time, intellectuals began to be proud of being black Africans.

During World War II, the official citizens of

Senegal supported the Vichy regime of Marshal Henri Pétain, which collaborated with the Nazis. Not surprisingly, the Vichy regime, which took on the Nazi racist policies, treated the blacks of Senegal very badly. The Senegalese were shocked and hurt to see this attitude from the French people they thought they knew and had trusted. They began to question their position in the French system. Eventually the French Senegal colony rejected the Vichy regime in favor of General Charles de Gaulle's Resistance Movement. Many black Senegalese soldiers, including Léopold Senghor, fought in World War II with the French Resistance.

CHANGES AFTER WORLD WAR II

After World War II, a liberated France revamped its policy toward its colonies. Senghor and the others had made the French more aware of the worth and validity of African culture. And the Nazi experience made the French more sensitive to the danger of attitudes of racial superiority and the values of democracy.

The French opened up Senegalese society and politics and allowed the organization of labor unions. Two Senegalese delegates, Lamine Guèye and Léopold Senghor, spoke in France's General Assembly of their pride and their desire for cultural and social freedom. The Communist and Socialist Parties were particularly sympathetic. Lamine Guèye was more influenced by the radicals. But Senghor, although a socialist, was more moderate, suspicious of any links with the Soviet Union through the Communist Party. The Soviet Union had used its World War II occupation of Eastern European countries as a pretext for taking them over permanently. Senghor saw a real danger for Senegal.

As delegates, Senghor and Guèye helped shape the postwar French constitution of 1946. Among other things, Senegal became an overseas territory of France, giving French citizenship to all Senegalese, not just the inhabitants of the four communes.

In the 1930s, Guèye had organized the Senegalese Socialist Party. Senghor had been a member, as well as being affiliated with the French Socialist Party. In the 1940s, however, Senghor began to feel there was a need for a party in Senegal with a more moderate, more democratic agenda. He created the Senegalese Democratic Bloc Party and a newspaper, *La Condition humaine (The Human Condition),* to promote his views.

Senghor began to build a coalition of other groups who were unaffiliated or unhappy with the Senegalese Socialist Party. He had strong support among Senegalese peasants, who were not well represented by the Socialists. In 1951, he ran against Guèye for a high office and won. He allowed a limited democracy to begin with moderate socialism but with strong ties to France.

MALI FEDERATION

Independence was the goal of all the African countries. Senghor believed a strong federation of the former territories in West Africa was the next step. Dakar would have been the natural choice as the strong center of this federation. Other leaders, such as Félix Houphouët-Boigny of the Ivory Coast, did not want to give up power in their own countries.

In 1958 Senegal tried to form a federation with the French Sudan (now Mali), Upper Volta (now Burkina Faso), and Dahomey (now Benin). But Dahomey and Upper Volta withdrew, leaving

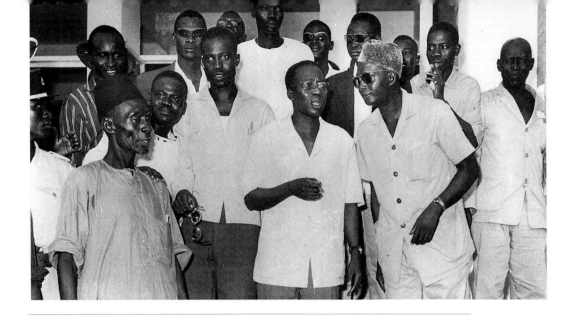

Senghor (front row, center) and his followers gathered in front of the National Assembly after voting to secede from the Mali Federation.

Senegal and Mali to form a new Mali Federation. The independence they requested from France was declared on June 19, 1960. Soon after, the other countries of West Africa also declared their own independence from France.

INDEPENDENCE

The Mali Federation lasted only a few months, however. A new constitution for a completely independent Senegal was created on August 25, 1960. Léopold Senghor was unanimously elected the new nation's first president, and Mamadou Dia, an economist, became prime minister.

Dia, a more radical socialist than Senghor, was not as popular. In 1962 he tried to use the national police to stop an election that he apparently was not going to win. But the army supported Senghor, the minor coup d'état failed, and Dia was imprisoned.

While most of the country supported Senghor, there was much

dissension, and it was difficult to keep order. Senghor allowed only one official party, but other unofficial groups were active.

In May 1968, great worker and student unrest in Paris led to sweeping social and political reforms in France. The demonstrations spread to Senegal. The protesters drew on the support of some Islamic brotherhoods in the countryside. Calm was eventually restored, and some governmental reforms were made.

Senghor held Senegal steady through the 1970s. But he was criticized for his ban on opposition parties. In 1974 he felt that the country was sufficiently stable to allow one opposition party, and several more followed.

Today, Senegal is divided into ten political subdivisions or regions: Dakar, Thiès, Louga, Saint-Louis, Diourbel, Fatick, Kaolack, Tambacounda, Kolda, and Ziguinchor. They elect a total of 120 representatives to the National Assembly every five years. At the head of each region is an elected governor.

As Senghor grew older he became even more popular. He began to be revered, in part because Africans accord great respect to old people. Senghor was seen as the father of his country, who had done a credible job in developing it. A world-renowned poet and intellectual, he brought pride and fame to Senegal—and to Africa. In 1980, he was ready to retire.

ABDOU DIOUF

Abdou Diouf had been Senghor's prime minister after Dia. He was Senghor's choice to succeed him, and Senghor had been grooming Diouf for the responsibilities of the presidency. Like Senghor, Diouf was educated in France, although he was a

Abdou Diouf met with U.S. President George Bush in Washington, D.C., in 1991.

"technocrat," not a poet. In open elections in 1983, Diouf won the popular vote. He has kept to the same democratic, moderate socialist course as Senghor. But he has encouraged even broader political participation, and there are more political parties than ever before. Political dissent is mostly peaceful and orderly, but occasionally violence has erupted. The peoples of Casamance—divided from the rest of the country by The Gambia—want to separate from Senegal, and have become violent. Bad relations with the Moors, who had lived in Dakar for many generations, erupted in race riots in 1989, after which most Moors left Senegal. There have been border conflicts with Mauritania.

In 1981 The Gambia needed Senegal's help to put down a rebellion. Senegal complied and an alliance was begun. The next year, the Senegambian Confederation was created for joint military defense and economic expansion. However, it, too, was soon disbanded.

Nonetheless, Abdou Diouf has increased Senegal's regional ties through commerce, trade, and joint programs. Many people feel that the many small independent countries in Africa have been a major stumbling block to the progress of Africa as a whole. Even as the Casamance region is seeking to separate from Senegal, Abdou Diouf is looking to unite Senegal further with the rest of West Africa.

Chapter 4

CITIES AND SITES

More than seven million people live in Senegal. Most of the population is concentrated along the Atlantic coast. One reason for this is that the coast has a more hospitable environment than the interior. It is cooler and more moist, making agriculture possible. Also, the coast has several port cities through which trade and commerce flow. Many large cities are situated either on or near the coast. Dakar is by far the largest city, with a population of about 1.7 million. Other cities of more than 100,000 people are Kaolack, Thiès, Rufisque, Saint-Louis, and Ziguinchor.

DAKAR

A look at a map of the Cap Vert Peninsula shows why this site was chosen for a port. The Cap Vert Peninsula juts way out into the Atlantic Ocean, and as it curves around and inward to the south, it creates a very sheltered harbor. The curve of land protects boats from the strong ocean currents that sweep down from the north. It was a "welcome port in a storm" for many sailing vessels coming down the coast of Africa.

Opposite: Dakar, seen here from a skyscraper hotel, is a thriving city and the focus of West African trade.

The railroad station in Dakar (left) is a central point for craftspeople to exhibit their products. Magazines from France as well as Africa are available at the international airport at Dakar (above).

The French first used Saint-Louis, the port to the north founded in 1633. But the Saint-Louis port became too shallow as sandbars built up around the river mouth. When it could no longer accommodate large ships, the French established a new port at Dakar in the mid-1800s. This new port would soon become a key center for the whole region. About that same time, the French began to build a network of railroads linking towns in Senegal with those in Mali, and Dakar was the center of this network. So, because of its geography, Dakar eventually became the capital of the French West African empire. It grew steadily in importance—commercially, intellectually, and culturally.

Dakar, the only Senegalese city with skyscrapers, matches the image of a modern international city.

A century later, when Senegal declared its independence from France in the 1960s, Dakar was the natural choice to be the capital of the new country. It is not as powerful today as it was when it was the capital of the whole French West African empire, yet it still exerts considerable influence in the region. Commercially, it is the busiest port in West Africa, serving Mali and Mauritania, and it is linked to other cities and regions by railways and new highways.

The whole Cap Vert Peninsula consists of a grouping of rocky plateaus, and much of Dakar is set on a particularly high plateau, so it benefits from the sea breezes, making it a pleasant location. The beautiful beaches around Dakar are appreciated by tourists and Senegalese alike.

Dakar has many different neighborhoods, both modern and traditional African. The French influence is still very strong, because Senegal is still very much tied to France as a trading

Beneath the skyscrapers are congested neighborhoods where traffic tries to squeeze into old, narrow streets.

partner and cultural focus. French is the official language of Senegal, although Wolof is used more often. With its bustling downtown areas, skyscrapers, and international airport, Dakar is an impressive, modern international city, the only truly modern city in Senegal.

The other major cities, while they have economic, regional, or historical importance, are pretty old-fashioned. They have no skyscrapers, and the simple, rustic buildings are often picturesque, but sometimes just run-down. Such cities underscore the poor economic conditions that are a reality of Africa. Dakar has plenty of those types of buildings, too, which provide a striking contrast with the impressive new high-rise buildings.

Dakar has many attractive tree-lined avenues, as well as beautiful, residential areas where wealthy Senegalese live—and there are many rich people in Senegal who live very well. The charming stucco houses are often in the colonial style, with balconies and interior courtyards, all covered with bright bougainvillea flowers. There are innumerable French-style

Women show off their flowers at the Kermel flower market by wearing them.

sidewalk cafes, superb international restaurants, and scores of sophisticated, fashionable people. Tourists enjoy walking around the area.

On the other hand, many, if not most, neighborhoods do not have electricity or a sewer system. There is a special neighborhood called the *Medina,* an Arabic word that generally refers to the "old town" or native part of a city which is otherwise modern. The Medina in Dakar is not terribly poor, but it is certainly not up-to-date.

Dakar has three major markets. The Sandanga Market is particularly picturesque. Designed in the Sudanese style, it looks a bit like an Arabic palace, or something out of the *Arabian Nights,* again underscoring the diverse cultural influences that make Senegal so intriguing.

Another market is the Kermel, which is more functional than picturesque. At both sites, local people can buy everything from fresh fish, vegetables, and flowers, to clothes and audio cassettes. Tourists can buy pottery, leather goods, or other souvenirs. The Tilene Market is in the Medina, so, not surprisingly, it carries more exotic items—including *gris-gris,* which is charms and potions for

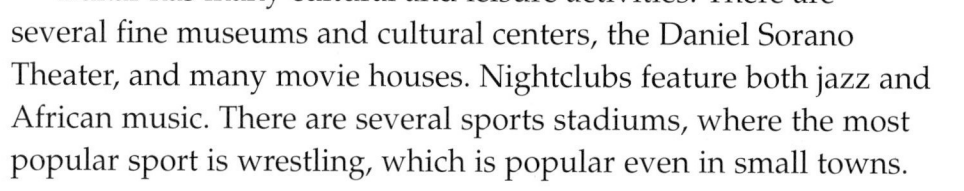

Left: Dakar's Grand Mosque was built in the
Moroccan style.
Above: Dakar's modern docks serve a large portion
of West Africa.

good luck or long life, such as monkey paws and owl wings.

As in many other countries around the world, people from Senegal's countryside often migrate to the city to find jobs, or simply to try and profit from the opportunities—or pleasures— they feel the city can offer them. In Dakar, these new arrivals live in huts, shanties, or barracks on the outskirts of the city, with no sanitary facilities, not even running water. As in large cities almost everywhere, there is more crime in Dakar than in the smaller towns, but it tends to be petty thievery, and not violent crime.

Dakar has many cultural and leisure activities. There are several fine museums and cultural centers, the Daniel Sorano Theater, and many movie houses. Nightclubs feature both jazz and African music. There are several sports stadiums, where the most popular sport is wrestling, which is popular even in small towns.

Wood carvings made throughout West Africa are sold in the art market at Dakar.

The University Cheikh Anta Diop, formerly the University of Dakar, attracts students from all over Africa, not just Senegal. A huge new International Conference Center provides modern facilities that draw many business and professional people.

Small and large Islamic houses of worship, called mosques, are found all over Senegal. The Grand Mosque of Dakar, built in 1964, is quite modern in style. Built with money given by the king of Morocco, it was designed to be similar to a mosque in Rabat, Morocco. Dakar also has a large Catholic church that can hold two thousand worshipers.

Because of its importance as a capital, there are many government and office buildings all over Dakar. And because of Dakar's importance as a port, there are many ships and cranes in its harbor, with depots for oil, groundnuts, and fish nearby. Dakar is the largest and best-equipped port between Morocco and the Ivory Coast, and the services provided to the ships contribute to the economy. The transportation system is efficient, with train, air, and highway routes leading out of and into Dakar's port.

The western tip of the Cap Vert Peninsula, Pointe des Almadies, is the most westerly point on the whole African continent. Many ships, deceived by its shallow reefs, have been wrecked there.

Special boats are used to collect the salt that crystallizes out of the exceedingly salty water of the Lac Rose. Huge numbers of birds are attracted by the lake.

Some are still visible. Now the Pointe is an attractive vacation setting, with a fashionable hotel complex. They even have a small oyster farm, just so diners in the restaurant can have fresh oysters.

To the north of Dakar, there are several picturesque places that are often photographed. One is the *Lac Rose* (the Pink Lake). The pink color of the lake is caused by the minerals in the water, which is ten times saltier than seawater. The Senegalese process this water to extract the salt. Birds, such as flamingoes, spoonbills, pelicans, terns, and many seabirds, abound.

Also up the coast from Dakar, there are many picturesque fishing villages. The people of Yoff belong to the Layène Islamic Brotherhood, and are often photographed on Fridays when they all wear their white robes.

Located a short drive from downtown Dakar, the city of Rufisque can be considered a suburb of Dakar. It wasn't always so, for Rufisque was one of the four original French communes that enjoyed special citizenship privileges. But as Dakar and Rufisque have grown, and transportation has improved, they have become linked in a kind of "urban sprawl." Economically important, Rufisque is known mostly for its large, profitable cement factory.

Students at Saint-Louis play soccer in their spare time. Throughout Africa, soccer is a vital sport both for playing and watching.

SAINT-LOUIS

Saint-Louis is only the third-largest city in Senegal, but as the capital of French West Africa in the nineteenth century, it played an important role in African history. That illustrious history is evident in its architecture.

Although in use as a port before, it was officially founded in 1659 and named for a king of France. Settlement began on an island where the Senegal River flows into the ocean, then spread to the mainland. The island was easily defended from rivals. European trade and involvement with West Africa grew from the seventeenth to the eighteenth centuries, and so did Saint-Louis.

However, Saint-Louis declined rapidly as Dakar grew. The city has been left pretty much as it was, giving it the nickname "New Orleans of Africa." The colonial architecture, with its wrought-iron balconies, shuttered windows, and beautiful well-established gardens, is reminiscent of New Orleans. Saint-Louis stands in sharp contrast to the modern style of Dakar. Many Mauritanians live in Saint-Louis, adding to its variety. Also, many churches reflect its religious diversity.

The cities of the Ferlo are important centers for groundnut production. These huts are used for storing the nuts.

CITIES OF THE FERLO

The fertile part of the Ferlo Desert has several large cities, which are mostly agricultural centers of distribution. In the western part of the Ferlo, the desert becomes more and more fertile closer to the Atlantic coast. Although the sandy soil dries up completely after the rainy season, it is highly productive when it is moist. The land between and around the cities of Diourbel, Kaolack, and Thiès is a key agricultural area. The first rail connections were established between these cities and to other places beyond Senegal, which contributed to their growth.

Diourbel is the name of both the city and the region around it. It is famous for its groundnut (peanut) production. And because groundnuts are so vitally important to Senegal's economy, Diourbel is very important indeed. Diourbel and Kaolack share the nickname of "groundnut capitals" of Senegal. Located near the

The cities of the Ferlo are primarily agricultural centers, especially for the production of groundnuts. The people above, who live near Diourbel, are tilling the soil around young plants. The men at the right are harvesting the nuts.

Sine River, on a major railroad link with Dakar, Tambacounda, and Mali, Diourbel is an important commercial hub. The major industries are food-processing plants, mainly based on the ground-nut production. It is also well known for its fine craftspeople who create bronze sculptures of the ancient kings (such as Lat Dior, the last Wolof king, and a very popular figure with the Senegalese), as well as wood sculptures, embroidery, leather work, and gold and silver jewelry. Diourbel is also an important religious center, with a large mosque.

Near Diourbel, on the railroad link to the north, lies Touba, a small sleepy town most of the year with a population of about 25,000. It seems to be a very ordinary market crossroads on the railroad, like so many others in Senegal, but it is the sacred city of an Islamic brotherhood. Once each year, about 250,000 pilgrims of the Mourides Islamic Brotherhood come from all over Senegal to celebrate Magal, the birthday of Amadou Bamba, a great *marabout*, or religious leader. They crowd into the town, or stay at campsites run by the brotherhood or in nearby towns. Touba bustles with the activity of traders and vendors as well as pilgrims. They begin to congregate in Touba and in nearby towns for several days before Magal, and celebrate all through the night.

The mosque at Touba, the Tomb of Amadou Bamba, is one of the most beautiful and impressive buildings in Senegal. The minaret is 285 feet (87 meters) high, the tallest in Senegal.

THIÈS

Just an hour's drive from Dakar, Thiès is one of the oldest cities in Senegal. It dates from the thirteenth century, and has been an important city to Wolof kings and Muslim leaders. Today, the railroad from Dakar splits at Thiès, going north to Saint-Louis and east to Diourbel and Mali. But in addition to its importance as a commercial rail hub, it is an important religious and cultural center. The Wolof at Thiès converted early to Islam, and Thiès grew to be an important center of religious learning. There are many mosques at Thiès.

Despite its history, however, neither Thiès nor the surrounding area is particularly attractive. A dusty, sprawling town surrounded by desert, people work in phosphate mines nearby, which help account for the city's importance. The cultural interest of Thiès lies in its arts and crafts, particularly in the unique tapestries that are

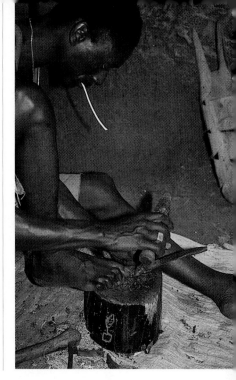

Hardwoods of the Thiès area, though difficult to obtain now, are used for fine carvings.

made there. At the government-sponsored workshop, artisans create wool tapestries from paintings created by Senegalese artists. Woven in brightly colored wool, they depict typical scenes of life in Senegal. The large ones can cost thousands of dollars.

Thiès used to be a center of precious African hardwoods such as ebony and mahogany. Regrettably, these fine trees were overused as firewood. The encroachment of the desert has resulted in less vegetation, and thus less firewood to cook with. Artisans wishing to use these fine hardwoods for carving must now import the woods from deep in the interior, where the supply is dwindling also.

KAOLACK AND THE MEGALITHS

South of the Ferlo, in the more fertile Sine-Saloum area, Kaolack is another important center of groundnut production and distribution. On the banks of the Saloum River, it is also on one of the oldest rail lines as well as on a modern major highway. A plant that evaporates seawater to produce salt is a major source of Kaolack's revenue.

Like Thiès, Kaolack is not a particularly attractive city, but it has a fine mosque of the Tidiane Muslims, and a particularly beautiful marketplace, a Sudan-style mud-based building with

A busy cotton mill in Kaolack produces great quantities of cotton thread.

oriental arcades and a large patio. The areas of the Sine-Saloum River Basin nearby offer some of the most beautiful scenery in Senegal, with lush, graceful, open forests, lagoons, sand islands in the river, mangrove swamps, and picturesque villages. The scenery in the Saloum Delta National Park is particularly interesting, and the park, a haven for birds, draws many tourists.

Near Kaolack are the mysterious megaliths of Sine Ngayene, which have long intrigued scholars. Scientists are not sure of the purpose or origin of the stones, nor do local ethnic groups have an understanding or explanation of them, either. Similar sites are found in various places in the Senegambia area. The stones, of varying sizes, are always arranged in lines or circles. There are more than 150 stones at Sine-Ngayene, spread out among ten small villages. One site has three circles of red iron-stone *stele* (flat, vertical stones) composed of about twelve stones each. Another has button-shaped stones and a lyre-shaped stone. Like the other stone circles found in Senegambia, they are a great attraction for scholars, as well as tourists who love mysteries!

Three Wolof women at the market in Tambacounda are dressed in traditional clothing. One carries a baby on her back.

TAMBACOUNDA

Even though Tambacounda has only about 20,000 inhabitants, it is the largest city in the eastern part of Senegal. It developed only after the railroad that goes to Mali was built. At the foot of the Fouta Djallon mountains, it is a stopping-off point for visitors to the great Niokolo Koba National Park, the largest in Senegal. The park covers over 800,000 acres (323,760 hectares) with many types of terrain, from grasslands to lush forest to marshes and mountains.

More than eighty species of mammals live in the park. Its wide variety of vegetation and terrain, coupled with the cooler moisture of the higher elevation, allows for a great diversity of wildlife, from the largest—over a hundred elephants—to the smallest birds, and over a hundred lions, as well as rare leopards, hyenas, and jackals. Among the smaller cats are the civet, serval, and genet. In

Exciting wildlife can be seen at Niokolo Koba National Park. The vervet monkey (left) is common, as it is throughout much of Africa. The elephants (above) are more scarce but making a comeback.

the rivers, there are hippopotamuses, turtles, and crocodiles that grow up to 10 feet (3 meters), and monitor lizards that grow to 7 feet (2 meters) in length.

Mahogany and kapok trees are plentiful along the rivers, and the trees are full of monkeys, such as the green vervet, or grivet, and red colobus, as well as some occasional chimpanzees. The grassland areas support great herds of grazing animals, such as the black antelope and the little duiker. The grazing animal herds are estimated to include several hundred thousand animals. More than three million migratory birds of more than three hundred species pass through the park. Near the rivers, marshes, and grasslands, storks, herons, spoonbills, and such weaverbirds as the buffalo weaver and blue-billed weaver can be seen.

Hunting is allowed in the area east of the park, where hunters can bag small and medium-sized game, such as antelope and

Ziguinchor is the main town in the Casamance region. The port area is shown, but there is a thriving market and colonial town nearby.

warthog. Tourists to the park often also come to see the colorful ceremonies of the Bassari people who live near Kedougou. They have several ceremonies during the year, and April offers the traditional initiation ceremonies, found intriguing by both anthropologists and tourists.

ZIGUINCHOR

Located on the south bank of the Casamance River, about 45 miles (70 kilometers) in from the Atlantic coast, Ziguinchor has experienced considerable growth in recent years. Because the river is navigable by oceangoing vessels, Ziguinchor was originally founded as a fort by the Portuguese in 1560. It later developed as a town under the French, and became quite prosperous. As the capital and main marketplace of the fertile, humid Casamance region, Ziguinchor has benefited from the natural resources of the Casamance, such as the farms, timberlands, and fisheries. There are some small industries here, such as sawmills, an ice factory, and a peanut-processing plant.

Ziguinchor's growth can be attributed also to the rise in tourism in the Casamance region. Ziguinchor is served by an airport and excellent roads. Tourists stop off there on their way to the resorts of the Casamance. It is a pleasant city, with broad

Dancers at a tourist resort in Casamance laugh at a tourist's camera.

palm-lined streets, and French colonial architecture. There are several markets that are a magnet for the peoples who live in the surrounding area—such as the Diola, Mandinka, and Tukulor, as well as the smaller ethnic groups who live in the forests and are rarely seen outside their villages. They all come together to buy or sell fish, produce, groundnuts, cotton, rice, spices, and palm products. Traders come from as far away as Guinea-Bissau, The Gambia, and even the north of Senegal and Mauritania.

Tourists often take pirogue trips up and down the Casamance River or travel to Basse Casamance National Park, an area of rain forests, savannas, and mangrove swamps. The beaches at nearby Cap Skirring are regarded by many as the finest in the country.

At Enamporé, the local people use a most unusual reservoir system, called an *impulvia*. It is the only system of its kind in Africa. Rainwater passes through the funnel-shaped roofs of buildings built especially for this purpose, and is collected in reservoirs, to be used in the dry season. The huts of this area are also remarkable, for they can shelter up to fifty people, as well as livestock and grain.

Chapter 5

PEOPLE
PAST AND PRESENT

Senegal is a small country, only about the size of Nebraska or South Dakota. The ethnic groups living in Senegal today have inhabited the region for many centuries. They have traded with each other, intermarried, made wars, and taken each other as captives. So the groups are well related by heritage, and their beliefs and customs often are similar.

Of all Senegalese customs, the social divisions—called *castes*—that were practiced for hundreds of years are the most distinctive. They are not typical of Africa as a whole, but they are very important in Senegal. The exact castes are a little different within each ethnic group. The caste system was abolished by the French, and is illegal under the present constitution. In the cities and among the educated Senegalese, group affiliation and caste are not as important as they are in the countryside. Yet, because family and heritage are so important, the ethnic group and the caste that one's ancestors were born into are still important in Senegalese society.

There are six main ethnic groups in Senegal—the Wolof, Serer, Peul, Tukulor, Diola, and Mandinka—with about twenty subgroups within them. They tend to live in specific areas, such as the desert, rivers, mountains, or forests. Very often, groups live

Diola people in the Casamance region celebrate an initiation rite for a young boy.

side by side with each other, sometimes in the same village. Most of the same groups are found in neighboring countries, such as Mali, Guinea, and Mauritania. Others, such as the Wolof, Serer, and Diola, are unique to the Senegambia region.

DOMINANT WOLOF

The Wolof make up over 40 percent of the Senegalese people, and are culturally dominant. The Wolof language is spoken by about 80 percent of the people. The Wolof, who are both respected and resented, tend to be a powerful majority in the cities. They are well educated, follow Muslim traditions, and hold most of the powerful positions in business and government.

The Wolof ethnic group is found only in Senegambia. Long ago, they lived in the northeast corner of Senegal and may have originated in Mauritania when the area was more fertile than it is now. In the fifteenth and sixteenth centuries, various groups of Wolof-speaking people were organized into a kingdom, which

Wolof women share the labor in their village of Meur Mbarick. Wolof houses and walls are often built of adobe brick.

This Wolof man is a member of the Presidential Guard.

began to conquer other people, making them pay taxes and demanding allegiance. They intermarried with neighboring Serer, Tukulor, and Peul peoples, acquiring some of their customs, and incorporating many of their words into the Wolof language. These other ethnic groups, however, have often resented the Wolof for their closeness to the colonial powers.

The Wolof were dominated by the Mali rulers during the Mali Empire. By the nineteenth century, they became powerful again, and their cultural dominance continues. Today the Wolof are found all over Senegal mingling with other ethnic groups. They have been at the forefront of change, and have helped promote groundnut cultivation.

SERER

The Serer are the next largest group, making up about 15 percent of the population. They live in the forested Sine-Saloum and Thiès area. Based on their oral traditions and their close relations with the Peul and Tukulor, it is believed that they originated in the Senegal River Valley with these ethnic groups. They left the region in the twelfth century when it came under

This Serer hut in the Thiès region has modern iron beds.

Muslim domination because they refused to convert. They continued moving southward to avoid Wolof domination, finally settling in the fertile areas where they are now. They have a reputation as very skillful farmers, using effective methods of irrigation and fertilization. Along the coast, they live by fishing. They often form large settlements, but their abundance has led to overpopulation, and they have had to move to other areas and seek jobs in cities.

Always independent, the Serer tended to resist outside influence and change, and thus did not trust their neighbors who embraced outside cultures. The Serer kept their traditional religions until recently when many converted to Islam. About 15 percent, usually the educated people who live on the coast, are Christians. Léopold Sédar Senghor was part Serer.

Left: A Peul woman wears her jewelry to market.
Above: A Tukulor man shows a string of prayer
beads he made.

PEUL AND TUKULOR

Several ethnic groups are united by language. The Peul and
Tukulor speak variants of the Pulaar language. They are also
physically similar. Together, they make up 23 percent of Senegal's
population. Historically, they have had close relations, often
intermarrying.

The Peul are also known as the Fulani by the English, and they
call themselves Fulbe (singular: Pullo). They are nomads who live
all over West Africa, southeast to Cameroon and east to Sudan.
Their origins were probably north of the Senegal River. Many have
settled around the middle valley of the Senegal River and in the
Casamance region. Others are nomads of the semiarid Ferlo. Many

Huts of both thatch and mud make up a Peul village near the border with Mauritania.

Peul live in villages among the Tukulor or the Wolof.

The Tukulor also had their origins in the north. They live mainly in the north by the section of the Senegal River valley called the Fouta-Toro. Other Tukulor live across the border in Mauritania, Mali, and Guinea. They are descendants of the Tekrur Empire people, who have mixed with many Serer and Peul people. They raise cattle, and those who live close to the river are farmers. With bad drought and economic conditions, the Tukulor have had to migrate in large numbers to the cities. The first group to convert to Islam in the eleventh century, they are very proud of their Muslim history.

DIOLA AND MANDINKA OF CASAMANCE

The Diola live in the fertile lower Casamance River area. They make up only about 7 percent of the population. They have lived

Left: *This Diola woman lives near Ziguinchor.*
Above: *Village women share their work pounding cassava, or manioc.*

in Senegal in the Casamance for hundreds of years, the longest of any group, although they probably originated farther north.

Unlike most other groups, the Diola have isolated themselves, and do not share many Senegalese customs. Very independent and democratic, they have never kept slaves or had a caste system of any kind. They never organized into large tribes or kingdoms. They do not form work groups and age groups. The heads of the groups are elected rather than being born to the job, as are many in Senegalese societies. Many Diola want to separate from the rest of Senegal.

Living in a fertile area, they are excellent farmers. Although some have recently become Christian or Muslim, most still follow their traditional animist religions. There are many subgroups, all of which live only in the Senegal area.

Unlike the Diola, the Mandinka are found throughout West

Africa, starting from the Gambia River through the Casamance down to the Ivory Coast, Guinea, and Mali. In Senegal, however, they live mostly along the Casamance River. The Mandinka are descended from the tribes of the great Mali Empire, with origins in a part of the Upper Niger River called Mandé (in present-day Mali). As the Mali Empire expanded, they spread to the Casamance, the Sine-Saloum, the Gambia, and then along the Atlantic Coast.

The Mandinka are self-sufficient farmers who prefer to trade with other Mandinka people in Guinea and Gabon. They have been Muslim since the jihad of the Mali Empire. The Mandinka also are called the Manding, Mandingo, Malinké, and Mandé. Another group, the Bambara of the Niokola Koba, is linguistically related. Together they make up about 6 percent of Senegal's population. Kunta Kinte, the hero of Alex Haley's *Roots*, was a Mandinka from The Gambia.

OTHER GROUPS

Other groups, although only 1 percent of the population or less, have a long and sometimes distinguished history. The Lebou live independently along the important Cap Vert Peninsula. The Sarakole are descendants of the Ghana Empire and live as traders all over West Africa. The Diahkanke of the northeast are an ancient trading people. The majority of the Bassari, Balante, Mandjaque, and Mancagne live also in Guinea.

Few Moors now live in Senegal because of border and economic disputes. Senegal's significant Lebanese and European minorities are responsible for much of the nation's trade and commerce.

A NEW ETHNIC VIEW

For a small, relatively poor country, Senegal has had a fairly significant influence on the rest of the world. That influence has been strongest in Africa and French-speaking countries. In general, Senegal is respected as a cultural and intellectual leader of Africa. The educated Senegalese are articulate, cultivated people by any international standards. More than sixty newspapers and magazines are published in Senegal, and many are distributed abroad. The Senegalese are often innovative critical thinkers.

Several people from Senegal have gained international prominence in politics, literature, history, and even films. Some, such as former president and poet Léopold Sédar Senghor, are admired by everyone. Others are more controversial, such as Cheikh Anta Diop, whose theories have nevertheless made historians and anthropologists everywhere reconsider their views. Both men have had positions in the forefront of major world movements, spearheading the way for change.

It should not be surprising that Senegal has produced such accomplished individuals. Senegal has been a place where people were encouraged to develop their minds. The Senegalese profited from both the French love of learning and the French policy of assimilation, or the absorption of colonial people into the French culture. Citizens who became educated and fluent in French could be appreciated for their mind and achievements, regardless of their color. That attitude helped create a positive self-image for the Senegalese, encouraging them to develop freely. However, many developed more freely than the French anticipated, learning to criticize and to question everything, including the French.

Poet and president Léopold Sédar Senghor (right) was born in the Christian community of Joal on the Petite Côte. Shown in the picture above is a Christian cemetery at Joal where fishermen who die at their work are buried.

SENGHOR AND NÉGRITUDE

Former president and poet Léopold Sédar Senghor is the most famous Senegalese. He would have been famous for his practical political achievements alone. But he also is remembered as a great poet and cofounder of a school of poetry that became a major world movement. At a time when few presidents can appreciate poetry, let alone write it, Senghor has been a true Renaissance man of the twentieth century.

Léopold Sédar Senghor was born in Joal on the Petite Côte in 1906 to wealthy parents. He was part Serer, Mandinka, and Peul. He was proud of his diverse ethnic and cultural heritage and liked to think of himself as representing almost everything that was essentially Senegalese. He was born Catholic, like most of the people in that area, and he remained Catholic all his life. Educated at Catholic schools, he was a gifted student. When he was sent to France to study in 1928, he excelled in his studies there, too.

Senghor spoke fluent French—as well as any Frenchman. He

Senghor saw the special beauty of African women and began to appreciate it instead of thinking that only European things and people could be beautiful.

eventually became an authority on French grammar and taught both Latin and French at *lycées* (something like junior college, but in those days, it represented considerable learning) in France.

In Senegal, he felt thoroughly French. But when he went to France, he experienced a great culture shock. There were few black people in France, and he felt isolated and homesick. He wrote frequent letters to his mother, and then he began to write poetry. Longing for his home and family, Senghor saw the scenes of his childhood more clearly. He wrote earthy, lyrical poems filled with longing for the savannas, rivers, and sounds of chanting at evening. He especially wrote of the warmth and beauty of African women—whether mothers, sisters, lovers, or strangers—and of his feelings for them.

When his poems were published in 1945, they showed mastery of the French language and of the exacting forms of French poetry. But they pulsated with the uniquely swinging rhythms of Africa. In 1948 he published *Anthology of the New Black and Malagacian French Poetry,* which included the works of other black poets. The anthology has become a classic.

In 1947 Senghor started a magazine, *Presence Africaine,* with Aimé Césaire of Martinique and Léon Damas of French Guiana.

The youth of African countries can take pride in their own heritage partly because of Léopold Sédar Senghor's role in changing the attitudes of people by his writing.

The poetry and essays they wrote began to be called *négritude*—the quality or attitude of blackness. The négritude movement became a forerunner of the "black is beautiful" idea of the 1960s and 1970s in the United States.

Senghor's political career began with his membership in the Socialist Party, where he made friends and earned respect. After the Nazis invaded France in 1940, Senghor joined the French Resistance. He actively supported General Charles de Gaulle who was directing resistance fighters from exile in England. Senghor was taken prisoner of war in 1940.

He was freed after the liberation of France in 1944, and began his political life. In 1945 Senghor was elected one of two deputies from Senegal in the French National Assembly. He was a powerful, articulate speaker, and his ideas helped shape the new French government and the status of former French colonies. In 1955 he was appointed a government minister—the first African in French history to hold such a position. Remarkably, during this time he was still writing and publishing poetry: *Chants pour Naët (Songs for Naët)* in 1948, *Ethiopiques (Ethiopian Things)* in 1956, and *Nocturnes (Nighttime Thoughts)* in 1961. In 1984 Senghor was admitted to the French Academy, an elite organization of writers. Senghor was the first black person to be admitted.

Upon Senegal's independence in 1960, Senghor was the natural choice to lead the country as president. The early years of independence were chaotic, and there were many challenges, from devastating droughts to huge oil-price increases to civil unrest. Senghor was able to keep Senegal on a course of peace and stability that has earned him the respect (and the envy) of other world leaders. His devotion to democracy and his rejection of communism and totalitarianism have been an example to other countries.

Senghor provided many government grants to establish and support the arts in Senegal. In part because Senghor was a poet, literature was favored. His government gave support to fledgling publishing companies, which published works in both Wolof and French. Many authors found world fame. The Daniel Sorano Theater was established to showcase works by Senegalese writers, musicians, and dancers.

The development of arts in Senegal favored literature also because Muslim tradition does not encourage the visual arts. Traditional Senegalese art consisted mainly of decorating masks, making pottery, and printing fabrics, although glass painting has recently become very popular. Under Senghor, traditional arts and crafts were encouraged, and the Dakar School of Fine Arts was established to train painters, sculptors, and tapestry weavers. The National Tapestry Works at Thiès has become famous.

Drums made of gourds are among the traditional Senegalese musical instruments.

OTHER WRITERS

After Léopold Senghor, Birago Diop is Senegal's most famous writer. But in addition to poetry, Birago Diop also writes stories that are drawn from Senegalese myths and legends. Born in 1906 near Dakar, Diop was a Wolof and a Muslim. His family was well educated; one brother was a journalist and author, another was a doctor. Birago Diop studied in Senegal and in France, eventually becoming a veterinarian. As an animal doctor, he traveled all over the Senegalese countryside, becoming familiar with the stories and customs of all the ethnic groups. He gave the name of the griot of his mother's family, Amadou Koumba, to one of his books.

Like Léopold Senghor, Diop's poetry is a synthesis of French forms and African feelings. On the one hand, his poetry shows him to be a master of French versification; his idols were Alfred de Musset, Victor Hugo, and Paul Verlaine. On the other hand, the content of his poetry is uniquely African, based on ethnic myths

Filmmaker and writer Ousmane Sembène traveled to the premiere of one of his films in New York in his traditional costume.

and stories, with mystic and animistic views of life and nature.

Women writers of Senegal have achieved prominence in recent years, too. Mariama Bâ, who published her first book in 1980, and Aminata Sow Fall, who first published in 1979, are widely read in Senegal. In contrast to Birago Diop, they write stories about real everyday life in Senegal, particularly about the concerns of women—sometimes practical, sometimes romantic. For example, *Such a Long Letter,* by Mariama Bâ, deals with polygamy, as a woman writes of her jealousies, frustrations, and longings.

The tendency among modern writers is to write about contemporary social problems, not the myths favored by Birago Diop. Nor do writers still feel the need to glorify their négritude, as Léopold Senghor did. Ousmane Sembène writes often about the problems of poor people. His films *Camp de Thiaroye* and *Xala,* based on his novel *Le Mandat,* have won prizes at prestigious international film festivals and have been distributed abroad. Unfortunately, filmmaking needed government support to continue. With a growing economic crisis in Senegal in the 1970s, support had to be cut, and filmmaking has not recovered.

To facilitate archeological research, Anta Diop started the first carbon-14 dating laboratory in Africa at the University of Dakar. The university was eventually renamed in his honor, University Cheikh Anta Diop. This is its new library.

CHEIKH ANTA DIOP

While Senghor and others were developing their ideas of négritude in the 1940s, Cheikh Anta Diop was beginning to develop his theories of the role of Africa in Western civilization. In 1974, he published his *African Origins of Civilization* in French. Drawing on his research in history, archeology, anthropology, and languages, he supplied evidence that the early civilization of ancient Egypt was "negroid," or black African. The Egyptian civilizations in turn shaped Greek and Roman civilizations on which all Western culture is based. In addition to presenting new evidence, Anta Diop states that white Europeans had deliberately ignored evidence of blacks and sub-Saharan Africans in Egypt.

Not surprisingly, the book created a great controversy among Egyptologists, historians, and archeologists, who refused to admit racial bias. They accused Anta Diop of his own racial bias for claiming too much credit for black Africans. Others have pointed out that previously whites had not recognized the importance of black history in any way. Controversy aside, interest in African culture and history is on the rise, thanks in large part to Anta Diop.

One of the daily tasks of most village women is to prepare flour for cooking.

Chapter 6

EVERYONE
HAS A PLACE

For all the people in Senegal, social life is extremely important. All live in close-knit, cooperative communities that share land and goods with each other, and portion them out according to rules.

People are born into traditional family structures that dictate everyone's rights and obligations. All know their exact lineage from both their mother's and their father's sides. The relationships among all those people are very important and precise.

In addition to having a place in a family structure, there is an "age" group for every stage of life—one each for children, adolescent boys, adolescent girls, women, men, and elders. These age groups are often work groups that function like mini-councils. They decide things together. Leaders are sometimes hereditary, sometimes elected. People are loyal to their age and work groups.

Then there are the Islamic brotherhoods (mostly for men, but some are for women, too). They unite people across ethnic and family lines. Although they exist primarily for practicing religious faith and learning, they can also function as work groups.

Social relationships are important because for the Senegalese, like most Africans, people are important, often more so than wealth or accomplishment. In fact, wealth is measured differently.

A market, such as this one in Toube Toul, lies at the center of each village.

For many Senegalese, wealth is measured in the number of cattle one owns. Cattle provide nourishment, they multiply, and they can be traded more easily than money. The number of people in a family is also a measure of wealth, and the Senegalese seek to have large families, which provide more people to help with work and to defend against attack. Each person is protected when young and cared for when old.

People are important and relationships are valued. They are also the greatest single source of pleasure, entertainment, and satisfaction in life. There is much warmth and affection between families and friends. Individual Senegalese may get lonely like everyone else in the world, but no one is ever alone.

FAMILIES AT HOME

Family relationships are different according to each ethnic group. The Senegalese have a heritage from the mother's line (matrilineal) or from the father's (patrilineal). They can inherit rights to land and cattle from either one (depending on the rules of the group), and children belong to and take the name of one or the other, also depending on the ethnic group. In the past, the matrilineal line was the most important, but as Senegal takes on more Islamic

Goats and the family share this enclosure in the village of Diemoul near Thiès. Observing the mother at her tasks teaches the girls things they will need to know in the future.

customs, this is changing to the father's line. In the former slave families, children always belonged to the mother, and the mother's heritage is still quite important.

In the villages, extended families live together in fenced-in compounds. Compounds consist of a main house and other small houses, with a courtyard in the center, and a house for any goats or livestock. Most Senegalese are polygamous—the men have more than one wife. Well-to-do men in cities may be able to provide a separate house for each wife.

In the center of the village there is usually a marketplace. The village is constructed around a water source of some kind, either a river or a pool. If the water dries up or the land becomes farmed out, the entire village must be moved. Houses are built of clay in arid zones, of wood and grass in fertile zones, and sometimes with scrap metal near cities. People sleep off the ground on homemade cots. The nomads of the north and the Ferlo live in tents as they travel from pasture to pasture. Most other Senegalese live in fairly permanent village settlements of perhaps two hundred people, but many in fertile areas live in groups of a thousand or more.

In Dakar and other cities, people often settle in areas similar to family and group compounds. They prefer not to live with strangers, although many single men who migrate to the cities must live without their families.

Time spent with others is important. And treatment of others requires a show of care and consideration. Senegalese are very polite. There are precise rules for greeting, which amount to a kind of ritual. Men usually shake hands and may continue to hold each other's hand as they speak. Then, slowly and unhurriedly, one begins to ask how the other person is, then how his family is, then individual members of the family—wife, mother, and children. He asks about health, work, and in general makes sure everything is all right. Then it is the other person's turn to inquire. This ritual takes some time to complete, but must take place before other practical—or even urgent—matters can be discussed.

Senegalese are light-hearted and warm. In some situations, with certain people they know well, they love to tease. Wolof are a little more reserved and are even thought to have a somewhat abrasive sense of humor. However, the jokes and insults they trade are all done in good spirit.

FOOD

Except during times of drought, Senegalese eat abundantly. They would rather eat the food they produce than trade or sell it. *Ceebu Jënn,* a Wolof rice-and-fish dish, is typical of the coastal and

*Above: By tradition, Senegalese men and women
generally eat separately.
Right: A country woman sifts grain for grinding.*

river areas, where fish is abundant. Each woman prepares food for her family and enough for any guests who might show up. She takes care to arrange the food attractively. Rice is put on a large flat tray, with vegetables and fish on top. Everyone eats from the same tray, using the right hand to press the rice and fish together. Reaching is bad manners, and the hostess will serve those who cannot reach the tray. There is a bowl of water for washing before and after the meal.

In the coastal cities, the French influence is evident. The often spicy, Senegalese-French cuisine served in restaurants is among the finest in West Africa. Millet or bulgur stewed with vegetables with a groundnut sauce is a staple of the poorest village people. It is served with milk and cheese if they have goats or cattle. Meat, such as lamb or chicken, is rarely eaten. Maize, beans, potatoes, cassava, green vegetables, and fruit provide variety.

Left: A large, old baobab tree shelters a woman from the sun as she waits for a bus.
Above: The staff of a Catholic mission give medicine to nursing mothers in a small village.

The baobab tree, which is found in every village on the savanna, or grassland, provides fruit, and its leaves also can be eaten. Many myths surround the baobab tree because of its many uses, as well as its strange appearance. Its sweet-smelling flowers are used in festivals, its fruits can be eaten or made into a drink, and its leaves are eaten fresh or dried. Powdered leaves and fruit of the baobab are used as medicine for rheumatism; the bark is used against malaria. Its often-gnarled trunk can grow to 30 feet (9 meters) in diameter and hold great quantities of water. When the baobab dies, it is made into a canoe because it floats. Sometimes the whole trunk is used as a coffin to bury a griot.

FROM CHILDHOOD TO OLD AGE

Unfortunately, it is not lack of food but ethnic taboos and customs that have denied certain foods to women and children, creating health problems for them. For instance, men are given

Children learn by watching their parents and other grown-ups doing their tasks, such as washing clothes (left). They also get plenty of time to play; the girl above is jumping rope.

most of the food, while women and children eat what is left. For this and other reasons, infant mortality is quite high in Senegal—40 percent of the children die before five years of age. Total life expectancy is low in Senegal. Average life expectancy is only fifty-five, although, of course, many Senegalese live to be much older.

In a society where people and family are so important (and so many children die), it is not surprising that children get a great deal of attention. Children are adored by everyone, not just by mothers. Men take the time to play with children, and showing affection is definitely not considered unmanly.

Mothers take their babies everywhere, caressing them, singing to them, massaging them, and breastfeeding them whenever they are hungry. Mothers continue to be close to their children into adulthood. In fact, the relation between mother and child is closer than between husband and wife.

Small children begin by playing games that imitate grown-up

Although Senegal has a tradition of education, children are unlikely to go to school very long. This school is in a Wolof village.

work. Little by little, they become helpful. Girls begin to help with the pounding of millet, which takes many hours. Boys follow their fathers and brothers into the field and may do a little weeding. Soon they become productive workers, for children start helping with work when they are very young. Boys and girls play with each other until they are about twelve, when they are separated into same-sex groups with others. The groups are very strong among traditional Senegalese, and they continue throughout life.

Although the law requires that children attend school for six years, many children do not attend. Neither children nor their families want children to leave the compound for any reason. Some villages have schools, but some children must stay at boarding schools. For those who do want education, the government has not been efficient in providing it. The children who go to elementary school, then to high school or university, are usually those who live in cities and are relatively wealthy.

It is disappointing that with Senegal's historical emphasis on

Girls dress in their finest traditional costumes to attend a wedding in Tambacounda.

intellectual achievement, the literacy rate is only 28 percent. Education, however impressive, is directed to an elite group, and has not helped the majority of Senegalese. Only 60 percent attend primary school, and only 15 percent attend secondary school.

MARRIAGE AND WOMEN

Among traditional people, young women marry around age nineteen, young men wait a little longer. The marriage is usually arranged by the parents, but the young people can choose, too. The young man's family must pay the young woman's family in money or cattle. If the couple divorces, the payment must be returned. Divorce happens but is looked down on. The people always remarry. The Senegalese cannot imagine why anyone would not be married. Even older women who are widows marry again, although they usually live with their married children rather than their new husband.

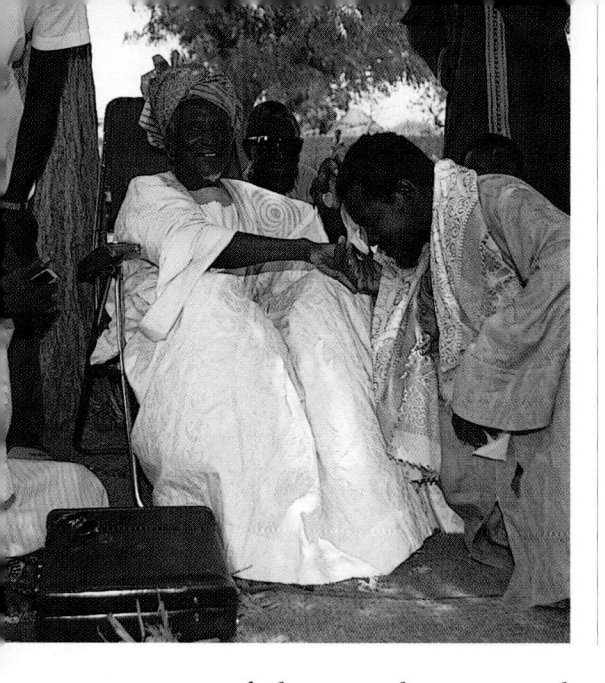

The oldest man in this village in the region of Thiès is listened to with great respect.

In most ethnic groups, children may belong to the father, but they live with their mother. A mother's children may have different fathers due to divorce or illegitimate birth, and each child's father may have several wives. So it's tricky for children to keep track of all their half-brothers and sisters, cousins, second cousins, aunts, and uncles. Yet they do, for it is quite important to them. They are bound to help these people, give them gifts at weddings and births, attend funerals, and may ask for help from these people when they need it.

The practice of polygamy is still popular. Many Senegalese follow the Islamic limit of four wives, others do not. Senegalese men say polygamy poses no problems, but Senegalese women don't always agree. In particular, the first wives usually resent other wives most, although subsequent wives don't mind—except that the first wife generally has more rights, particularly when she has the man's first child.

In many ways, the status of women is difficult. The laws have not provided them the same rights as men. However, visitors to Senegal eventually come to see Senegalese women as powerful in their own right. Because they are so close to their children, they continue to exert considerable influence when the children become adults. The opinions and wishes of the women's work groups carry great weight, and the men usually take care to appease them.

Many Senegalese men say that women are stronger than men, which gives men an excuse to take more food. In some groups, women do much more of the work than men.

Visitors to Senegal describe the women as warm, smiling, and secure. In a country that feels the real wealth is in the children, women as bearers of children have the highest status of all; and Senegalese women know it.

Older people of both sexes are respected. Older people also belong to age groups—usually with the same people they were with as children. When they express their views, either individually or collectively, their wishes are generally the final word on the subject. It is the council of elders that settles disputes in the villages, from accusations of theft to farming rights.

ISLAM

Statistically, between 70 and 90 percent of Senegalese people are Muslim. There are varying degrees of adherence to the faith, however, and not all Senegalese Muslims are very strict. Many practice an Islam that is blended with their traditional animist religions; it is quite different from Islam practiced elsewhere.

Islam was founded by a Saudi Arabian, Muhammad, in the sixth century. Islam requires that its followers accept certain basic tenets, and the writing in the Qur'an, or Koran, is the authority. But interpretation of the Qur'an, like the Bible for Christians, is open to differences, and some rules are observed more than others.

The practice of Islam in Senegal is organized around different brotherhoods. They are based on theology and sometimes on ethnic affiliation. The brotherhoods were powerful political forces,

Children are more likely to go to a religious school, such as this one held in a village hut, than to a regular school. Here, they learn Arabic so that they can read the Qur'an.

and in recent times, the political aspect of the brotherhoods has become stronger and stronger.

The Qadiriya is the oldest brotherhood in Senegal, dating from the twelfth century in the Arabian Peninsula. By the nineteenth century, Qadiriya spread through Senegal as far as the Mandinka of the Casamance. Rather strict, it emphasizes law and learning. The Tidianes brotherhood was established in the late eighteenth century, and was spread by the Moors to Senegal. Tidianes tend to be an educated elite who live in cities. The most famous leader was the Senegalese national hero Al Haj Omar, who converted his fellow Tukulor and neighboring Wolof, Peul, and Sarakole of the Senegal River area to Islam. The spiritual center of the Tidianes is in Fez, Morocco. The brotherhood has several branches that are organized along hereditary ethnic lines.

The Mourides brotherhood was founded in the nineteenth century by Amadou Bamba, a morally strict mystic. Wolof at all levels, including slaves, joined. Then, as now, the Mourides tend to be poor farmers, former slaves, or orphan boys who find support in the brotherhood. Agricultural work forms a part of their belief, and they work on communal farms where all the goods are given to the religious leaders. The brotherhood is seen by many as exploitation of the poor and uneducated. Because the Mourides require absolute dependence and obedience from followers, they are a powerful political force in Senegal.

Other brotherhoods include the Layènes, a small brotherhood living on the strategic Cap Vert Peninsula. They wear all-white clothing and are often photographed in their picturesque robes.

ANIMIST RELIGIONS

On the surface, it is hard to understand how the Senegalese can reconcile elements of the old animist religions with the practice of Islam. After all, Muslims must repeat, "There is no god but God," and there is no place in Islam for other deities. However, Islam recognizes devils, angels, and evil spirits, and spirits form the basis of the animist religions. Also, the animist religions believe in the existence of one all-powerful being who lives in the sky, but who is not, however, involved in earthly or human undertakings. In Islam, the supreme being can be worshiped directly.

Many Senegalese are strict Muslims, yet they also appear to follow some of the animist beliefs. For instance, most Senegalese—the devout Muslim, the intellectual, and the animist—wear little amulets around their necks. These contain charms to ward off evil spirits and also may contain verses from the Qur'an. Muslim fishermen and farmers still perform old rituals to ensure a good

Left: An animist religious leader writes the words for a charm.
Above: Spirits can be called on through rituals involving masked dancers.

catch or a good crop. Also, when someone is sick, even devout Muslims may turn to old prayers and rituals.

Few Senegalese are pure animists. However, understanding animist beliefs can help in understanding the Senegalese way of experiencing life and nature. In animist belief, people have a living, intimate connection with nature and their ancestors. The animists believe that a number of forces control events on earth, and they must try to influence these forces to help, not harm, them. Spirits can live in trees, rocks, or water. There are even spirits of villages or homes. Basically people are not afraid of the spirits, but only appeal to them for help. Spirits must be worshiped and sacrificed to help people avoid disease, death, and crop failure.

Spirits can be called up by ceremonies and men wearing masks. They also believe in the power of witches to bring harm to people through evil spirits. Evil spirits can take animal forms. Night is a dangerous time because spirits prowl and can invade the body unless stopped by amulets. Animists also believe that the souls of their dead ancestors help them with everyday events. Ancestors can influence spirits, too. Some groups practice possession rituals, where they believe that spirits and dead ancestors can inhabit women's bodies, allowing spirits to speak and act through the women. Many animist beliefs came to the New World with the slaves who were settled around the Caribbean. They became the foundation for *Vaudou*, or voodoo.

CHRISTIANITY

Christians make up only about 5 percent of the population. Most are Catholics who live along the coast where European influence has always been strongest. There are a few Protestant missions run by Westerners.

The teachings of Christianity were harder to adapt to African ways of life than Islam, so it never became widespread. The attraction of Christianity was usually because of their Western-oriented schools. Because of this education, many Senegalese Christians have held high places in government. Senegal's first president, Léopold Senghor, was a Christian. As with Islam, Senegalese Catholic liturgies, prayers, and music have a very African flavor, and dancing is sometimes common during worship.

The cathedral in Dakar is the center of Christianity in Senegal.

As Senegal moves into the twenty-first century, its economy will probably remain a combination of agriculture and small business, such as the village shop above, and the labor-intensive work of binding and embossing books in the Yoff village in Dakar, below.

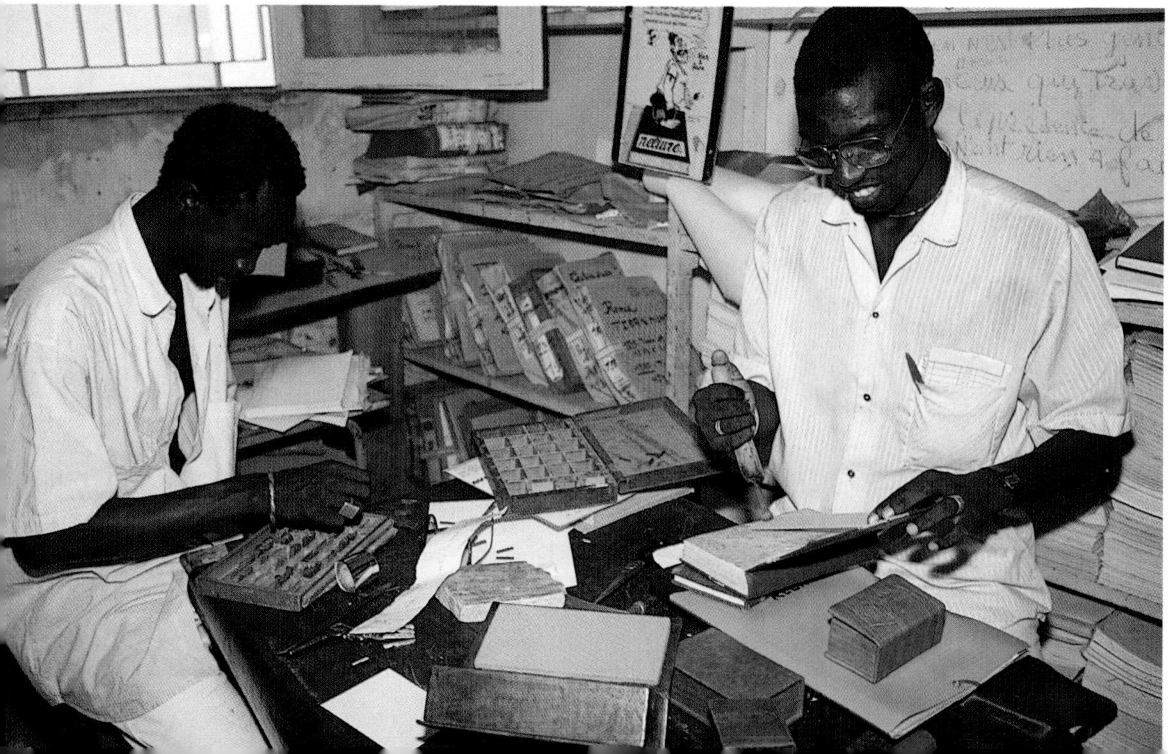

Chapter 7

NEW CHALLENGES

Like most of the other African countries that declared their independence from colonial powers in the 1960s, Senegal began with a spurt of optimism and energy—and over-confidence. The people were full of nationalism and pride, and eager to take over the reins of the industries and government agencies that the French had formerly controlled. They were sure they could do everything just as well, or better, than the French, for they cared more about Senegal. They felt that the French had been holding them back from developing their full potential.

The confidence and ambition of that post-independence period were tremendous. The Senegalese felt they could turn Senegal into a modern, industrialized society that would be successful in every way. As so often happens, energy and enthusiasm did accomplish a great deal.

The 1970s, however, brought an abrupt halt to growth and expansion. Most importantly, there was a worldwide oil crisis that was devastating to developing countries. OPEC, the Organization of Petroleum Exporting Countries, decided to raise the price of oil considerably. While this made the oil-producing countries wealthier, it was very damaging to other developing countries. Oil and gas shortages followed. Americans and Europeans waited in long lines to get a limited amount of gasoline at very high prices.

Dakar remains a vital port for the whole of West Africa, where many cargo ships come in (above). It's been even more important in recent years when grain had to be imported because of severe periods of drought. The men at the left are bagging grain shipped from the United States.

Unfortunately, poorer countries, such as Senegal, simply could not afford to pay higher prices for gas and oil. As a result, car, truck, train, and plane transportation was either reduced or was shut down completely, and with it, commerce and industry.

The high oil prices were catastrophic for the weak economies of the developing countries. Senegal was forced to borrow large sums of money from banks, international agencies, and foreign governments. Then they had to use all of their available money to pay back these debts, while interest accumulated, and the debt grew larger. There was no money left for many essential things, let alone the kind of progressive expansion they had so happily envisioned in the 1960s.

Matters were made worse in Senegal by long droughts, which forced the nation to import large quantities of food. This increased the debt to foreign countries, mostly to France. Unfortunately, the drought also permanently damaged the fragile topsoil.

In the 1970s and 1980s, the Senegalese government was obliged to keep on borrowing money from the World Bank and other countries just to finance everyday survival. And because of political promises made to the people, the government continued to borrow to fund ambitious social programs. Money also had to be borrowed to support Senegal's industrial development, which was doing quite poorly and proving to be very costly.

A NEW APPROACH

When Abdou Diouf became president in 1980, he turned his attention to Senegal's troubled economy. Swift industrialization had been a failure, and idealistic socialist programs had proved too costly. It was time for a new, more practical approach. Abdou Diouf wished to make Senegal more self-reliant and able to develop many small businesses. As president, he began to encourage a free-market economy that had less government involvement in business and industry. He soon began offering incentives to develop business and agriculture. He also cut government spending, including spending for the arts which were so dear to Léopold Senghor, and he reduced the number of government employees.

More and more, Senegal was accepting that it could not afford to neglect its agriculture sector and its land in favor of industrial development. Competing with Europe was no longer a priority. A major goal of President Diouf has been to make Senegal self-sufficient in terms of agricultural production, so that it doesn't have to import food.

While the labor of agriculture is still done in simple, old-fashioned ways (above), the Senegalese are learning to use modern methods such as the use of pesticides (left).

Although growing enough food on their own soil to feed their own people is a priority, the Senegalese know that some of their food products have an enormous potential for greater export—the abundant seafood, for instance. The shores off Senegal are a rich source of seafood, and shrimp and lobster can be frozen and exported all over the world. Peanut oil and phosphate rock are major exports, too, but they are subject to the rise and fall in market prices. Senegal's dependence on peanuts has meant that when there is a drought, or when prices are down, they lose a great deal of revenue. To lessen their dependence on groundnuts, they are starting to encourage production of other crops, such as sorghum, millet, rice, corn, beans, sweet potatoes, and cassava (manioc).

In the 1990s, most Senegalese still lived off the land. About 70 percent of the people were farmers. Most of Senegal's farmers are "subsistence" farmers, who are able to grow enough food to feed themselves and their families, and if the crop is abundant, sell or

This clothing factory is one of the small, privately owned companies that the Senegalese government is encouraging.

trade the rest. But there are also some large cooperatives and landowners, which the government encourages because of the efficiency of production.

THE PRIVATE SECTOR

Of the remaining 30 percent who were wage earners, most had jobs with the government (60 percent) and only 40 percent had jobs with privately owned companies. Another goal of Diouf has been to reduce the number of government employees and have them work instead in the private sector. This is difficult, to say the least, in a country of entrenched ethnic loyalties and allegiances. People feel obliged to help out their relatives and allies by giving them jobs, or even by creating jobs for them. They see nothing wrong with this.

Although Senegal's private sector is not comparable to that of developed countries, Senegal has more industry than other West African countries. The most important industry is peanut-oil processing, but other industries include fish canneries, a sugar refinery, a tobacco factory, a textile plant, a brewery, an auto assembly plant, chemical plants for the phosphates, and a cement manufacturing plant at Rufisque. Most of the industry is clustered around the Cap Vert Peninsula.

The future will call for the Senegalese to take advantage of their own talents and resources. The shop at the left features handmade musical instruments. The phosphate plant above mines the mineral for use in fertilizers.

The shipyard at Dakar is a huge operation that provides repair and storage facilities for vessels. Dakar is also an important financial center for the whole West African area, with many banks and financial institutions. The salt-production plant at Kaolack is successful, there is some iron-ore mining near the Falémé River, and several minor gum arabic-processing plants operate.

The development of tourism has helped Senegal's economy by bringing much-needed money into the country.

Diouf's stringent policies (and good rainfall) eventually put Senegal in a better position, compared to the drought and the oil-crisis years. Senegal has experienced a good growth pattern. In 1989 Senegal's gross domestic product—the sum of everything it produces—was growing at a rate of 6 percent a year. This is an excellent figure, but unfortunately is was not enough to keep up

Tourists are attracted to the amazing wildlife at Djoudj and other national parks. Tourism will be increasingly important in the future.

with payments on the enormous debt the nation incurred in previous years. This growth does not take into account Senegal's poor trade balance, either. Senegal still imports more than it exports. It needs items such as food, consumer goods, petroleum, machinery and transport equipment, which it imports mostly from France, Nigeria, Algeria, Thailand, and the United States.

THE NEW WORLD ORDER

Senegal has made many changes in its direction since independence. It is still a socialist democracy, but it has had to learn to accommodate business by actively encouraging a capitalist free-trade economy. It has had to learn to be agriculturally self-sufficient and to take care of the land so that more of this precious resource is not lost to the encroaching desert.

In recent years, two new factors have required Senegal to become even more self-sufficient. One was the breakup of the former Soviet Union. Senegal did not have significant ties to the Soviet Union. However, like many developing countries, it tended to use the threat of alliance with a communist country to get more foreign aid from Western countries. This is no longer an option.

Senegal still receives considerable aid from France and other countries. But the money now is given on a humanitarian level, not in order to lure an undeveloped country away from the influence of communism. Senegal fears that this kind of aid may dwindle or disappear altogether.

The second factor is France's closer economic ties with the European Community. France has made a series of trade agreements with other European countries. As France's trade alliance with other European countries becomes stronger, Senegal worries that its own alliance with France will inevitably be weakened and its economic privileges will disappear.

In fact, by the early 1990s, most of the countries of the world were in the process of developing or strengthening their own regional trading blocs, forming special arrangements with their neighbors. As France was strengthening its ties to the European Community (and giving up some of its independence), the United States, Mexico, and Canada were moving to strengthen and develop trade among themselves, as were countries of Southeast Asia. Senegal, too, has been increasing economic ties to other West African countries, and will no doubt continue in that direction, making the nation less dependent on France and the West.

Indeed, many Africans feel that they would be better off with even more self-sufficiency. They have depended for too long on Western aid, Western ideas, and Western solutions. Borrowing money from the West to industrialize and become an African

Senegal strives to be in touch with the world. President Senghor (above) spoke at the United Nations in the late 1970s. A Peul village (right) has TV antennas and solar-energy panels on its houses.

version of Europe had not worked. Their first priority must be taking care of their land, and, secondly, developing a simpler economy based on their historical strengths, and not on the kind of industrialism that works in the West.

With this acceptance of their self-sufficiency has come a new optimism and a relaxed confidence among the Senegalese people. There seems to be a satisfaction in returning to the land and making it productive. They gladly embrace the West, learn from it, and share with it, but they no longer judge themselves by European standards, or feel it necessary to keep up with or compete with the West. After several decades of independence, Senegalese have entered a new phase in their growth, which some people have called Afro-centrism—that is, from now on they will focus on being Africans in Africa.

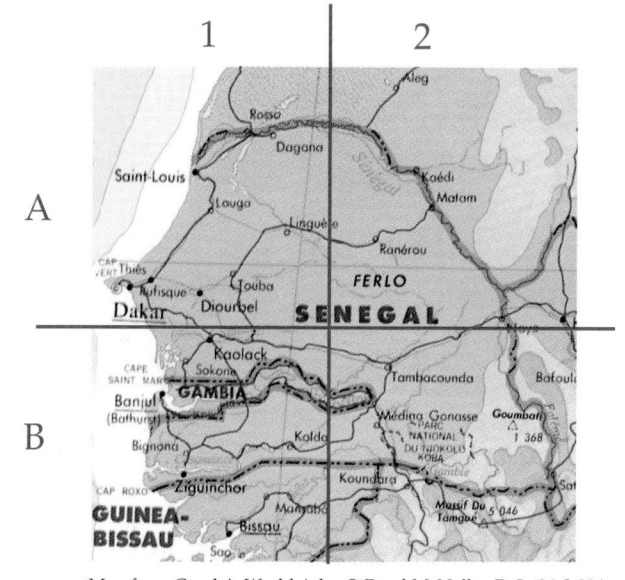

Map from Goode's World Atlas © Rand McNally, R. L. 96-S-224

SENEGAL (The Gambia is not labeled)

Bignano	1B		Matam	2A
Cap Roxo	1B		Medina Gonasse	2B
Cap Vert	1A		Naye	2A
Casamance (river)	1B		Niokola Koba N.P.	2B
Dagana	1A		Ranérou	2A
Dakar	1A		Rufisque	1A
Diourbel	1A		Saint-Louis	1A
Falémé (river)	2B		Saloum (river)	1B
Ferlo	2A		Senegal (river)	1A,2A
Gambié (river)	2B		Sokone	1B
Goumbati (mtn)	2B		Tambacounda	2B
Kaolack	1B		Thiès	1A
Kolda	1B		Touba	1A
Linguère	1A		Ziguinchor	1B
Louga	1A			

MINI-FACTS AT A GLANCE

GENERAL INFORMATION

Official Name: République du Sénégal (Republic of Senegal).

Capital: Dakar

Government: Senegal is a multiparty republic with one legislative house, the National Assembly of 120 members. The president is head of the state and the prime minister is head of the government. The president and the cabinet members are elected for five-year terms by citizens over 21 years of age. The Socialist Party of Senegal has been in power since Senegal's independence in 1960. The Supreme Court is the highest judicial court. For administrative purposes, the country is divided into 10 regions.

Religion: Senegal is a secular country. The constitution guarantees freedom of religion to all. However, some 90 percent of the population follows Islam. The Islamic brotherhoods, headed by *marabouts* (religious leaders), are the most common religious organizations. Some 5 percent of the population is Christian, mostly Roman Catholic. The Diola, Mandinka, and Tukulor people have resisted both Christianity and Islam, and still practice traditional animistic religions.

Ethnic Composition: Almost all Senegalese are black Africans. Several ethnic groups and subgroups with their own languages and customs live in Senegal; among them, the Wolof is the largest (45 percent), followed by Serer (15 percent), Peul (Fulani) and Tukulor, jointly comprising 23 percent, Diola (7 percent), and Mandinka (6 percent). People in the north are related to the Moors of North Africa. There are some Lebanese and European minorities.

Language: French is the official language, and all official business is conducted in French. Wolof is the most widely spoken (more than 80 percent) and understood language. Most of the ethnic groups speak Wolof and also their own language.

National Flag: The national flag has green, yellow, and red vertical stripes. A green star, the symbol of African freedom, is in the center of the flag on the yellow stripe.

National Emblem: A shield is divided into two vertical halves with one side displaying a golden lion on a red background, and the other side displaying a green baobab tree and two wavy lines (the Senegal River) on a yellow background. The shield is enclosed by black and white palm branches around a green star at the top of the shield. The national motto, *"Un-Peuple—Un But—Une Foi"* ("One People—One Goal—One Faith") is on a scroll at the bottom of the shield.

National Anthem: *"Pincez Tous Vos Koras, Frappez les Balafons"* ("Pick up your Koras, Strike the Balafons."

National Calendar: Gregorian.

Money: CFA franc of 100 centimes is the official currency. The CFA franc is the currency of French-influenced West African countries, and is tied to the French franc. In October 1996, 518 CFA francs were worth one US dollar.

Membership in International Organizations: African, Caribbean, and Pacific Countries (ACP); African Development Bank (AfDB); Customs Cooperation Council (CCC); Economic Commission for Africa (ECA); Economic Community of West African States (ECOWAS); Franc Zone (FZ); Group of 77 (G-77); Nonaligned Movement (NAM); United Nations (UN).

Weights and Measures: The metric system is in force.

Population: 1996 population estimates 8,610,000 with 113 persons per sq. mi. (44 persons per sq. km); about 58 percent live in rural areas and 42 percent in cities.

Cities:
```
Dakar . . . . . . . 1,729,823
Thiès . . . . . . . 216,381
Kaolack . . . . . . . 193,115
Ziguinchor . . . . . . . 161,680
Rufisque . . . . . . . 138,837
Saint-Louis . . . . . . . 132,444
Mboure . . . . . . . 106,046
(Based on 1994 population estimates)
```

GEOGRAPHY

Border: Mauritania is to the north, Mali to the east, Guinea to the southeast, and Guinea-Bissau to the south. The Gambia extends eastward inside Senegal.

Coastline: 310 mi. (499 km) along the Atlantic coast. The Cap Vert Peninsula is the farthest western point of Africa in the Atlantic Ocean.

Land: Except for the foothills of the Fouta Djallon mountain range in the southeast, Senegal is very flat. The southern part is called the Casamance. The dry, scrubby desert land in the north becomes gradually more humid toward the south. The Ferlo is a sandy area between the Senegal River and the Vallée du Ferlo River; this semi-arid region is used by the nomads as pasture. A belt of sand dunes, swamps, lagoons, and river estuaries marks the coastal area; these mangrove-filled saltwater marshes in the coastal zone provide excellent fishing. The Atlantic coast region is divided into the Long Coast, or *La Grande Côte,* and the Short Coast, *La Petite Côte.*

Highest Point: 1,634 ft. (498 m) in the southeast.

Lowest Point: At sea level.

Rivers: The major rivers are the Senegal, the Gambia, the Saloum, and the Casamance. Because the terrain is quite flat, rivers generally branch out into many tributaries near the coast and produce very marshy and swampy areas. The Senegal River Valley is about 10 to 25 mi. (16 to 40 km) wide, but it shrinks considerably during the hot summers. The Senegal River floods its banks once a year and provides fertile soil, silt, and water for agriculture.

Forests: About half of Senegal is under forests. Teak and mahogany trees and bamboo are found in the south. Raffia palms, oil palms, and mangroves are abundant on the coasts. In the drier regions, seasonal grasses, small bushes, and different kinds of acacia trees survive with a minimum of rainfall. Nomads move in search of grass for their livestock; this overgrazing has resulted in severe deforestation in northern Senegal.

Wildlife: Wildlife includes several large and small animals such as antelopes, crocodiles, chimpanzees, and elephants. The Niokolo Koba National Park has elephants, leopards, antelope, hyenas, wild dogs, jackals, hippopotamuses, water buffaloes, crocodiles, monkeys, chimpanzees, and porcupines; hunting is allowed in the eastern part of the park. There is a wide range of birds in Senegal including herons and storks. The Oiseaux du Djoudj National Park is a bird sanctuary with ducks, pelicans, spoon-bills, egrets, cormorants, storks, and pink flamingos. Saloum Delta National Park is a haven for many birds. The Langue de Barbarie National Park on Saint-Louis island is protected for sea turtles. Much wildlife has been wiped out by hunting and cultivation.

Climate: There are two distinct seasons, winter and summer. Winter lasts from November to May and is very dry; summer lasts from June to October and is also the rainy season. Except for June, when rain tends to be abundant, the summer is hot and humid. The highest amount of rain falls in the south, ranging between 60 and 72 inches (150 to 180 centimeters) annually. Annual temperatures range from 71° F. (22° C) on the coast to about 84° F. (29° C) inland. Senegal suffers from periodic droughts that turn more and more grassland into desert. Droughts have permanently damaged a lot of land by depleting the fragile topsoil.

Greatest Distance: Northwest to southeast: 429 mi. (690 km).
Northeast to southwest: 252 mi. (406 km).

Area: 75,955 sq. mi. (196,722 sq km).

ECONOMY AND INDUSTRY

Agriculture: Some 12 percent of the land is under cultivation, providing work for about 70 percent of the people. Groundnuts, or peanuts, is the chief cash crop; other cash crops are cotton, dates, palm oil, and fruits. Food crops include rice, millet, sorghum, and corn. People plant millet or groundnuts after the flood waters recede and harvest the crop in a few months. The *impulvia* is a unique irrigation system used in southern Senegal where rainwater passes through the funnel-shaped roofs of buildings and is collected in a reservoir to be used at a later date.

Fish are plentiful year-round. The most common fish are swordfish, perch, catfish, tuna, marlin, sea bass, sailfish, barracuda, sharks, oysters, crabs, and crawfish. Some dolphins and manatees are also found in the nearby waters.

Mining: Senegal has a few known minerals but only phosphate is mined in commercial quantities. Salt is extracted from the *Lac Rose* (Pink Lake) and also from seawater near Kaolack. Some iron ore is mined near the Falémé River.

Manufacturing: Senegal enjoys a much larger industrial sector than most West African countries. Peanut processing, food and fish processing, sugar refining, saw milling, textile, brewery, ship repair and storage, chemicals, and auto assembly are the chief manufacturing activities. There is a small petroleum refinery for imported petroleum. There is a cement factory at Rufisque. Shrimp and lobsters are plentiful in the coastal waters, and are potentially important for a canning factory that will freeze and export fish products to international markets.

Transportation: The transportation system is well developed and consists of 562 mi. (904 km) of railroads and 8,873 mi (14,280 km) of roads, of which about 30 percent are paved. Major cities are linked by road and most villages are linked by unpaved paths and waterways. Public transportation consists of buses, taxis, and minivans. Dakar is one of the busiest ports in Africa; it also serves Mali and Mauritania. The international airport is at Dakar.

Communication: Some sixty newspapers and magazines are published in Senegal, almost all in French. One daily newspaper has 50,000 circulation. Radio stations broadcast both in French and local languages. In the early 1990s, there was one radio per 9 persons, one television set per 133 persons, and one telephone per 123 persons.

Tourism: Tourism is promoted by the government. Most of the tourists are from Europe, especially from France. *Pirogue* (canoe) trips up and down the Casamance River are popular with tourists, as are visits to the tropical forests, savanna, and mangrove swamps.

Trade: Chief imports are machinery and transportation equipment, petroleum products, coal, rice, dairy products, pharmaceutical and paper products, and consumer goods. Major import sources are France, Ivory Coast, the United States, Nigeria, Italy, Thailand, Japan, Spain, and Germany. Chief export items are petroleum products, canned fish, phosphates, fresh fish, peanut products, shellfish, and cotton. Major export destinations are France, India, Mali, Italy, Iran, Ivory Coast, the Netherlands, and Spain.

EVERYDAY LIFE

Health: The Senegalese in general have good health. Both Western medicine and traditional medicines are used to cure diseases. Major causes of death are malaria, tetanus, meningitis, and tuberculosis. Life expectancy at 54 years for males and 56 years for females is low. The infant mortality rate at 68 per 1,000 live births is higher than in many other African nations. There is a severe shortage of physicians in the country, especially in rural areas. In the early 1990s, there was one physician per 15,000 persons and one hospital bed per 1,000 persons.

Education: The education system is based on the French model and French is the language of instruction. Education is compulsory for six years, but many children do not go to school. About half of the children attend primary school, with just 15 percent going on to secondary school. Most schoolchildren are from urban areas. The University of Dakar, now named the University Cheikh Anta Diop, is the country's only institute of higher learning. In the early 1990s, the literacy rate was about 30 percent.

Holidays:
New Year's Day, January 1
Labor Day, May 1
National Day, April 4
Christmas, December 25

Some Islamic holidays, such as Mauloud and Tabaski, fall on different days each year as they are based on the Islamic lunar calendar.

Culture: Senegalese culture is influenced by the French. A majority of authors still write in French, such as the former president Léopold Senghor, who is a world-renowned poet. The Daniel Sorano Theater in Dakar shows works by Senegalese writers, musicians, and dancers. The Tomb of Amadou Bamba at Touba is one of the most beautiful buildings in Senegal. The mysterious megaliths of Sine-Ngayene are large stones in lines or circles; these stone arrangements have long intrigued scholars.

Society: The society is made up of several ethnic groups of varying caste systems.

Although abolished by the French and made illegal by the government, a caste system is still followed by most people. Family and heritage are very important for Senegalese people, and these traditions are kept alive by adhering to the caste system. Most ethnic groups live in close-knit, cooperative communities that share land and goods with each other. Wealth is measured in the number of cattle one owns and number of people in one's family. Islamic brotherhoods are the dominant social organizations. They unite people across ethnic and family lines and function as religious and work groups. The Wolof are well educated and hold powerful positions in business and government. The Diola have always been democratic in organization and have never kept slaves or had a caste system of any kind.

The Senegalese follow heritage from both the mother's line and the father's line. Historically, heritage from the mother's side has been more important. Most men have more than one wife. Divorce occurs frequently. Children are adored by parents, grandparents, and relatives. Marriages are often arranged by the parents; the groom must pay money or cattle to the bride's family. Older people are respected, and they help to raise young children in the family. Almost all Senegalese, including Christians and Muslims, wear a little amulet to ward off evil.

Handicrafts: Senegalese traditional handicrafts are beautiful; they include bronze and wooden sculptures, embroidered items, leather work, and gold and silver jewelry. Carved wooden masks are the most famous traditional handicrafts of Senegal. Others include clay pottery, and fabric and glass painting. The brightly colored wool tapestries are made at Thiès, created from original Senegalese paintings.

Dress: Traditional clothing is popular in rural areas, but Western-style clothing is the norm in the cities. Senegalese men wear loose cotton trousers and loose-fitting robes called *boubou*. The women wear bright-colored, long, loose robes and elaborate turbans. The Muslims of the north wear long, loose robes covering most of their bodies, as required by their religion. Southerners wear very few clothes, sometimes just shorts, as humidity and temperatures are high in the south.

Housing: In cities, apartment buildings are becoming popular with middle-income families. Dakar has numerous high-rise buildings and charming rows of bungalows where rich Senegalese live. The poorer sections do not have electricity, running water, or a sewer system. Rural houses have mud walls and thatched roofs, or are made of wood and grass in fertile areas. Some rural huts in the southern areas are large and can accommodate more than 50 people at a time plus their livestock. The average village has 200 people; extended families live together in fenced-in compounds with a courtyard in the center and a house for goats or livestock. The nomads live in tents and move from pasture to pasture with their livestock.

Food: Rice, millet, or corn is the staple food. Most popular dishes are chicken stew, fried fish, and peanut sauce. *Ceebu Jënn* is a rice-and-fish dish. Rice is generally put on a large flat tray with vegetables and fish on top. Food is eaten from this common tray with the right hand only. For poorer village people, a millet stew with vegetables and groundnut sauce is the staple. Chicken or lamb is eaten very rarely. Other food items include beans, sorghum, potatoes, cassava, green vegetables, and fruits. Flowers, fruits, and leaves of the baobab tree are part of the everyday diet. Muslims do not eat pork.

Sports and Recreation: Wrestling is a favorite spectator sport and pastime. Soccer is the most popular sport; other games include basketball and jogging. There are several sports stadiums in Dakar. People in cities enjoy movies and videos.

IMPORTANT DATES

13,000 B.C. — First known record of people living in the Senegal region.

800 B.C. — The nomadic tribes start to build permanent residences.

140 B.C. — Greek explorer Polybius visits the Senegal coast; he writes about slavery, and trade of gold, salt, copper, iron, and glass beads.

A.D. 141 — The Romans rule northern Africa; they draw the first known map of the Senegal area.

A.D. 11th century — The Almoravids (Muslims) bring their armies into Senegambia.

1443 — Portuguese explorer Nuno Tristão reaches the Senegal area; he explores the Senegal River.

1465 — Trade between local chiefs and the Portuguese begins for gold and slaves.

1560 — The town of Ziguinchor is founded by the Portuguese.

1570 — The first French explorers arrive in Senegal.

1617 — The Dutch are the first foreign nation to establish a permanent trading settlement in Senegal.

1633 — The official Senegal Trading Company is authorized by the French government; French have the monopoly on all trade in the region.

1659 — Saint-Louis is founded and named for a king of France.

1661 — The English charter a British trading company.

1807 — Slavery is outlawed by the British.

1818 — The French explorer Gaspard-Theodore Mollien discovers the sources of the Senegal and the Gambia rivers in the Fouta Djallon mountains. The French abolish slavery—but not in their colonies.

1848 — Thirty years after abolishing slavery at home, France prohibits slavery in its territories in Africa.

1854 — General Louis Faidherbe is appointed governor of the French colony of Senegal.

1860 — Religious leader Al Haj Omar is defeated by the French.

1882 — France makes Senegal a French colony.

1895 — Senegal becomes part of French West Africa. The last armed rebellion against the French ends with the defeat of the Wolof King Lat Dior. Senegal become part of French West Africa, an official federation of the French colonies.

1914 — Blaise Diagne becomes the first Senegalese and the first African elected to France's National Assembly.

1945 — Senghor is elected as one of the two deputies from Senegal in the French National Assembly.

1946 — The postwar constitution of France extends French citizenship to all Senegalese.

1947 — Senghor starts a magazine, *Presence Africaine;* beginning of the *négritude*—the quality or attitude of blackness—movement.

1955 — Senghor is appointed a government minister in France—the first African to hold such a position.

1958 — Senegal and Mali form a federation with the French Sudan (now Mali), Upper Volta (now Burkina Faso), and Dahomey (now Benin); Upper Volta and Dahomey withdraw from the federation; Senegal and Mali form the Mali Federation.

1959 — Senegal requests independence from France.

1960 — Senegal withdraws from the Mali Federation and declares independence from France. A new constitution is created; Léopold Senghor is elected president.

1962 — Prime Minister Mamadou Dia tries to use the army to stop national elections, and he is imprisoned; the office of the prime minister is temporarily abolished.

1963 — A new constitution is promulgated.

1964 — The Grand Mosque is built in Dakar with financial help from Morocco.

1968 — A state of emergency is declared due to student and worker protests.

1973 — Senegal suffers from a severe drought. Diplomatic relations are broken with Israel and Guinea.

1974 — Mamadou Dia is released from prison; Senghor allows one opposition party.

1975 — Three political parties are authorized.

1978 — Senghor is re-elected president.

1980 — President Senghor retires voluntarily; Abdou Diouf becomes president.

1981 — The Gambia and Senegal agree on a confederation of the two states as Senegambia; it will have one monetary system, one president, and one military force.

1982 — The Senegambia Confederation is created.

1984 —The Casamance area, which wants to secede from Senegal, starts a violent civil disturbance. Senghor is admitted to the French Academy.

1989 — A border dispute erupts between Mauritania and Senegal over farming rights along the border; most of the Moors leave Senegal.

1990 — Ethnic violence continues against the Senegalese in Mauritania and against Mauritanians in Senegal.

1993 — President Abdou Diouf is re-elected.

1995 — The country is rocked with violent political protest; six police officers are killed.

1996 — Senegal and China break diplomatic relations as Senegal establishes trade links with Taiwan.

IMPORTANT PEOPLE

Michel Adanson (1727-1806), a French botanist; explored the Senegal interior for five years and published *Natural History of Senegal* in 1757.

Mariama Bâ, writer; her first book was published in 1980; works include *Such a Long Letter.*

Amadou Bamba, a mystic and a great Muslim leader of the Mourides brotherhood; his birthday is celebrated with great festivities at Touba.

Mamadou Dia (1910–), an economist and a radical socialist; elected Senegal's first prime minister in 1960; he tried to stop elections in 1962 and was imprisoned till 1974.

Blaise Diagne (1872–1934), the first African to be elected to the French Parliament.

Birago Diop (1906–), short-story writer; after Senghor, he is the best known Senegalese writer.

Cheikh Anta Diop (1923–) , a social reformer and educator; in his book, *African Origins of Civilization* (published in French in 1974), he contends that essential qualities of Western civilization came to Greece through Egypt, and the earliest Egyptian civilization was dominated by a black African ethnic group; he also contends that, due to racial bias, Western historians have undervalued contributions of the black people; he started the first carbon-dating laboratory in Africa at the University of Dakar; the university was later renamed University Cheikh Anta Diop in his honor.

David Diop (1927–60), an internationally recognized poet.

Abdou Diouf (1935–), prime minister from 1970 to 1980; became Senegal's president after Senghor in 1980; he was re-elected as president in 1993.

Louis Faidherbe (1818–89), French general and governor of the colony of Senegal from 1854 to 1864; his progressive rule was marked by numerous reforms and developments; he established free schools and health services, and a newspaper for the Senegalese; he constructed the first metal bridge at Saint-Louis, and promoted export of groundnuts.

Aminata Sow Fall, writer; her work was published for the first time in 1979; she writes about everyday life in Senegal.

Lamine Guèye (1891-1968), Senegalese delegate to the French National Assembly; promoted the cause of cultural and social freedom of the Senegalese society and organized the Senegalese Socialist Party in the 1930s; lost the election to Senghor in 1951.

Youssou Ndour, contemporary musician, drummer, composer, singer, and band leader; well known for his West African music style.

Al Haj Omar, a religious leader of the Islamic Tidianes Brotherhood; he fought a *jihad* (holy war) with the French in northern Senegal in the mid-1880s; he converted his followers to Islam.

Ousmane Sembène (1923–), writer and filmmaker; he writes about poor people and their problems; work includes *Xala* and *Camp de Thiaroye.*

Léopold Sédar Senghor (1906-), president of Senegal from 1960 to 1980; also a world-renowned French-language poet and intellectual; in 1984 he became a life member of the French Academy—the first black African to receive that honor. He retired to live in France.

Abdoulaye Wade, the leading opposition leader in the 1990s.

Compiled by Chandrika Kaul, Ph.D.

INDEX

Page numbers in **boldface type** indicate an illustration.

About the Author

Margaret Beaton, a native of Chicago, earned her bachelor's degree from Northeastern Illinois University and also did graduate work in French literature at the University of Chicago. She began her career in publishing and advertising.

In 1973, she moved to Paris and worked on the staff of UNESCO, the United Nations Educational, Scientific, and Cultural Organization. For six years she helped implement programs in education, science, culture, and human rights around the world. The experience of working on an international team, as well as her travels in Europe, Africa, and Egypt left her with a lively interest in international affairs and a commitment to furthering goals of international understanding.

After her return to Chicago, Ms. Beaton taught briefly, and then worked as a writer and consultant in publishing, direct marketing, and fund-raising.

Senegal is her second Enchantment of the World book for Children's Press. Her first book, *Syria,* was published in 1988. She has also written *Oprah Winfrey,* a biography for the People of Distinction series.